Getting Elected

Getting Elected

✦

Winning Local Elections

Thomas F. Renk

iUniverse, Inc.
New York Lincoln Shanghai

Getting Elected
Winning Local Elections

iUniverse books may be ordered through booksellers or by contacting:

iUniverse
2021 Pine Lake Road, Suite 100
Lincoln, NE 68512
www.iuniverse.com
1-800-Authors (1-800-288-4677)

ISBN-13: 978-0-595-39667-2 (pbk)
ISBN-13: 978-0-595-84073-1 (ebk)
ISBN-10: 0-595-39667-4 (pbk)
ISBN-10: 0-595-84073-6 (ebk)

Printed in the United States of America

This book is dedicated to
Karen, Courtney, Michael and Kate.
My Inspiration, my life!

"It is not the critic who counts; not the man who points out how the strong man stumbles, or where the doer of deeds could have done them better. The credit belongs to the man who is actually in the arena, whose face is marred by dust and sweat and blood, who strives valiantly; who errs and comes short again and again; because there is not effort without error and shortcomings; but who does actually strive to do the deed; who knows the great enthusiasm, the great devotion, who spends himself in a worthy cause, who at the best knows in the end the triumph of high achievement and who at the worst, if he fails, at least he fails while daring greatly. So that his place shall never be with those cold and timid souls who know neither victory nor defeat."

—President Theodore Roosevelt

Contents

Foreword

I know a gentleman who lives down the road about 12 miles from me. He was a great teacher at a rural high school southwest of Chicago, Illinois where he taught history and civics, and was the high school wrestling coach taking his teams to the state championship a number of times. In 1980, he was encouraged by his family and friends to run for the Illinois General Assembly to represent his District in Springfield, the State Capitol. He did get his name on the ballot but lost in the Primary election. Just before the general election, the designated Republican candidate who was expected to win suffered a stroke and was unable to stay in the race. This small town history teacher was asked to step in on short notice and went on to win his first election.

He served his District with distinction for the next six years at the state level and then was asked by his party to step into a race for the US House of Representatives in 1986. He won that election and has served ever since as the Congressman in the Illinois 14th District. In 1995 his party encouraged him to take on a leadership position as Deputy Republican Whip in Congress, and then in late 1998 he was elected by his Republican peers to become Speaker of the House. Since then he has sat third in line for the Presidency of the United States. I am proud to call him my Congressman, and friend, J. Dennis Hastert.

My reason for telling you about this national political leader is that he is just a normal guy from Yorkville, Illinois. One day about 24 years ago he was asked and decided to get more actively involved in his community's affairs. He was just a local citizen who decided to participate in his local government by running for office. He stepped forward to volunteer his services, perhaps like you are doing! There are thousands of people out there just like Denny Hastert, ordinary citizens living quiet lives, who are interested in becoming more politically involved, to make it a better place to live and raise their families. This is happening all over America.

In the fifty U.S. States there are 3,113 counties that each have hundreds of local governmental units within their physical boundaries. When you do the math, you easily have over 500,000 local elections up for grabs every couple of years. These local units of government include: city and municipal councils, village boards, school districts, county commissions, parishes, fire protection districts, Library boards and rural townships. There are also numerous other types of elective office depending on state law, local history and custom. All of these governmental units have one thing in common; they have embraced the democratic principles our forefathers conceived of over two hundred twenty-five years ago; they govern themselves. These communities draw upon their own citizenry to provide leadership and manage local affairs, and determine how they will be developed and managed.

There is a famous quote that embodies this principle of self-government. A number of governmental leaders have embraced these words in speeches and comments, but the comment can truly be attributed to President Abraham Lincoln. He said:

"Democracy is the government of the people, by the people, and for the people."

That is what this book is all about, government by and for the people in local elections. Ten years ago it was estimated there were over 537,000 elective offices posted nationwide. There are probably 50,000 new elective offices created since then, as new communities are developed and incorporated, additional jurisdictions are created within existing units of government, and towns and villages expand their political needs within their communities. The number of elective offices averages out to over 200 + elected positions per county. In urban metropolitan counties that number is considerably higher. And daily there are many more elective offices being created as new communities spring up and unincorporated areas form new local units of government to deal with urban sprawl and residential growth. In my area there are six unincorporated jurisdictions that are actively exploring incorporation to take over local government affairs.

With varying terms of office, these elective offices are filled each year with local citizenry. And the people running for these local offices are usually first time candidates, not experienced politicians. Most of these political novices have little knowledge and understanding on how to proceed, and are often unsure of where to seek guidance to become viable candidates. They have no idea how to comply with election regulations, or how to accomplish their goal of winning office. Again, that is what this book is all about.

When I first ran for public office in 1976, I thought I would go to the library and find a whole shelf of books dedicated to this political process. But that wasn't the case. I found books on "The Making of the President", and how to get elected to Congress, but my initial plans were somewhat more localized. I tried the major bookstores and ran into the same problem, there weren't any books on getting elected locally. I quickly realized I was on my own in uncharted waters and I had no idea of how to proceed.

The first time I ran for office I guessed my way through filing nomination papers, got my name on the ballot, and then quickly lost in the primary election six weeks later. My first political race was over before it really got started. So I tried again two years later, and promptly lost again. But in each of these short-lived political campaigns I began to learn about the real process of how to manage a campaign, how to fund a race, how to become visible in the community, and eventually how to win.

Through personal trial and error I learned many campaign lessons I will share with you. Over the past twenty-five years, I realized that this accumulated knowledge and political insight might be useful to other citizen-candidates venturing into this public arena. Over the years I collected notes on scraps of paper and cocktail napkins while trying to determine why I had won or lost. Then I began to have visions about a "How To" book, which could offer a fast start for a campaign. I hope this book will serve as a such a guide for you, saving you time, money and effort so you can win your election the first time!

The fact that you have found this 'how to' book would suggest you have already committed to this two hundred year old American celebration of democracy. When and if you make the decision to actually get involved, I'm sure our forefathers and the signers of the Declaration of Independence will applaud your interest and willingness to embrace their principles of freedom of choice. I can almost hear them cheering you on, pounding their walking sticks and swords in the chambers above. Good luck!

Who Are These People?

"The most important political office is that of the private citizen."

—Louis Brandeis

In most cases the people who decide to run for public office are ordinary folks, like yourself, the neighbor next door, the concerned parent at the PTA meeting, or the guy around the corner who borrows your tools. They are individuals that for any number of reasons have decided to get involved. Personal motivations can be as simple as being angry about some law being proposed; a desire to become more pro-active in local affairs; a desire to protect family and the quality of life; or perhaps a desire to craft the laws to make their hometown a better place to live.

So why do we have government in the first place? Many people might say that it is just another way for someone to get in the way of our individual rights as free men and women in a democratic society. I have heard government explained as the collective process of managing and coordinating large-scale community challenges and problems, issues and service demands, that people would not otherwise be able to handle or provide for themselves as individuals. President Jimmy Carter once said,

"Government is a contrivance of human wisdom to provide for human wants. People have the right to expect that these wants will be provided for by this wisdom."

A good example of an important human need and large-scale concern is the critical need public safety. Most people demand that there is general order in their lives and that their families can be safe and protected. At the local level this takes the form of good laws for the benefit of all, a strong police force and dependable fire protection. Hundreds of years ago, personal safety for your family involved a shotgun, but that isn't the case today. It is much more complex.

1

Police and fire protection is a very necessary fact of communal life as people gather and congregate in villages and cities throughout the country. Such close proximity brings all sorts of challenges in trying to take care of one another. Public safety has become a complex and expensive process, one that individuals cannot fund or manage by themselves. Local governmental units must step in and coordinate such services for the common benefit of all. Otherwise we would still have the lawless old west delivering six-gun justice. Today we need local government to coordinate these kinds of services for the benefit of the general public.

Another good example of a large-scale government service is the need for a safe and sanitary continuous source of water for personal consumption, and business use. A hundred years ago you could go the stream and get your own water unworried about what might have been dumped upstream. Today, water demands are huge and potable water production has become a very necessary service of local government. And once there is safe and potable water, then there must be a safe and dependable means of delivering it to people, and a parallel sanitary means to dispose of sewage and waste by-products to prevent disease and sickness.

You shouldn't drink the water from the stream anymore and can't get rid of waste by throwing it over the fence or burying it in the backyard, at least not in urban areas. This is where local government has had to step in because the costs of seeking viable sources of water, purification, treatment, delivery, fire capacity, and the costs of waste processing are astronomical. In my community a new Water Tower and well is costing over twelve million dollars. And citizens of these communities become elected officials to make all the decisions that go into these costly planning and delivery efforts to provide such services.

The democratic form of local government can best be described as people voluntarily coming together to provide services that they cannot afford to individually provide for themselves. No single person can build a personal water system, or a sewage treatment facility without adversely affecting their neighbors and the environment. People come together because of need, to solve problems that are bigger than they can handle individually. Government brings order where chaos once reigned.

Coordinating these complex processes of local government is where the action is. Local government is all about effective management of bread and butter issues that impact you and your family every day. Managing these functions is a fascinating democratic process that you can become a part of, to shape your community's future. But to do so you have to know how to get elected.

Why This Book?

This 'How To' book was written to assist all first-time candidates interested in getting involved in the process of governing. In most cases, the average citizen has little first-hand knowledge of the complicated process of government, the elective process, and the rules and requirements they must abide by.

Participating in the elective process can be a frustrating process if you don't know what you are doing, where to look for direction and answers to basic questions, who to turn to for support, and how to bring home a win. It takes a lot of commitment and a good amount of physical effort to win, even at the local level. You will need to understand the nuances and legalities of the elective process, and how to be effective with limited resources. Politics is a tough game that has all sorts of written and unwritten rules, which can get you into trouble quickly.

Over the years, I've been involved in eight local elections as a candidate. I have also worked on the campaign committees of other candidates in their quest for public office. I've navigated these uncharted waters as candidate and as campaign manager. I've learned the hard way because there was no book like this available. I wish there had been because it would have saved me countless hours and money. You can learn from my mistakes and save yourself lots of time.

This book will offer guidance, and at a minimum, suggest things you should think about before you rush into any campaign. There are many requirements you will need to review and consider. This book will discuss reporting responsibilities; point out how to find competent assistance, and offer practical tips on all sorts of minutia learned the hard way. Finally it will offer election-tested strategies to better utilize your time and effort to beat your opponents. Don't share this book with your opponents until after you have won the race. Then pass it along, or better yet tell them about the book website for their own copy. Keep yours for the next election.

A Word of Caution

From state to state, election and campaign rules and regulations can be quite different from one another, requiring specific filing deadlines, reporting responsibilities and financial accountability. Without knowledgeable forethought and an overall election plan you may be finished before you really get started. Many of the state and federal procedures and requirements will seem like roadblocks for the novice candidate simply because you get lost in the shuffle. All of these requirements occur while short-term deadlines are looming, and other candidates are getting their campaigns rolling. Many potential candidates give up just trying to wade through the campaign requirements. Let me help guide you on this exciting journey!

State Election laws, qualification requirements, and filing procedures differ from municipality to municipality, county to county, state to state. Never presume the information and rules presented in this book are complete for your specific jurisdiction or state. You will need to seek out the specific requirements you must run under and pay attention to them.

All of these campaign suggestions and comments should only be used as guidelines to pose questions in your mind, to identify potential issues and to explore problems you may run into in your election. This book will allow you and your campaign committee to ask the right questions and have a good idea of where to look for the answers.

It is important that you seek out solid information on all of the local election law requirements to protect yourself and your campaign. I suggest finding an attorney and see if they will join your campaign committee. They can offer good counsel that will help carry you through the campaign.

You should involve other people in this whole campaign process as well, so you have extra eyes making sure that you are doing all the right things, meeting deadlines, making good decisions. We will talk about your campaign committee and campaign chairman being part of your team, working as your inner circle of counselors. You should get them involved in looking at all the rules too. The more eyes you have researching these matters the better chance you will meet all the requirements and deadlines.

The Clerk, Your Best Resource

The best source for all the specific local election law information you will have to deal with is your Village, City, or County Clerk. The county clerk coordinates all unincorporated area activity. In some states it may be a Supervisor of Elections that is charged with managing the official documents for your candidacy. These individuals are the official keepers of all the information concerning elections. Don't be afraid to visit their office and ask questions you may have early on. Answering questions about local election law is part of their job description and I have always found these individuals to be a capable resource.

Over the years, I have also found the city or village clerk to be one of the most cooperative individuals in local government. The clerk comes into contact with the public all the time and they are used to being the communication link between the public and the various local government offices and departments. The clerk is your most important source of good election information to get the whole process started. If they do not know the answer they will know where to get the information. Always ask for specific information for the particular public office that you are seeking. Then ask additional questions and advise the clerk this is your first time running for public office. They will be happy to assist and show you the way. Don't be embarrassed to admit that you are a rookie and don't understand the elective process, because half the people running will be in the same boat. Most clerks started the same way and can readily help you through the many challenges you will face. They are public servants, just like you hope to be. First, it's their job, and second, you could win the election and become one of their elected supervisors. They want to make a good first impression too!

As a voter citizen in your community (I'm assuming you already registered to vote), and a first-time candidate, you can obtain all sorts of free guidance and good advice by not being shy. Admit you are a rookie by saying, "I'm new at this candidate game, are there other things that I should be aware of? Am I missing anything?" And then gently ask the same questions again in another way to make sure you are covering all the bases and getting the most pertinent information you will need to move forward. If the clerk doesn't know you are a first-time candidate, they will presume you know all the rules and regulations and will only respond to what is specifically asked. I know many past candidates who missed a required financial or filing deadline, because they misunderstood a comment, or misread a document written in government legalese. They were out of the race before they got started. Ask questions. Be pleasant about it, but be persistent. Being a novice candidate can actually work to your advantage.

Promises, Promises

Getting Elected is meant to offer basic counsel concerning the many practical matters you will have to consider as a candidate. None of this election campaign process and strategy is brain surgery, but it must be carefully reviewed if you want to be successful, which is the whole point of exposing yourself to all this effort. A campaign takes a lot of energy, time, resources and commitment. Here's what we will talk about throughout this book:

- **Funding your campaign** without using **your** money.

- **Building an effective network of campaign workers** to spread the word on your behalf.

- **Designing campaign materials** for distribution at various meetings and going door-to-door.

- **Creating and using a campaign website** to gain visibility.

- **Developing an effective publicity campaign**, to obtain good press coverage and utilize the media to present your campaign.

- **Psychologically defeating your opponents** throughout the campaign.

- **Identifying community issues, and staking out positions** to take the high ground in debates and public forums.

- **Raising money and getting the most bang with your funds.**

- **Orchestrating an effective door-to-door campaign** to develop a strong presence everywhere in the district (even if you don't have one).

- **Coordinating lawn signage** for tremendous exposure.

- **Building coalitions and strategic alliances** to generate votes.

- **Identifying the real voters and getting them to turn out on Election Day.**

Lots of promises, I know, but the concepts in this book are tried and true formulas for success. These approaches have been tested in the political trenches of many campaigns, some successful, others not. But in each race valuable lessons were learned the hard way. By trying and testing concepts I was able to learn what works and what doesn't work. When I won an election, I tried to figure out what made the difference, what had we done differently, and what actually motivated people to vote for me. When I did not win an election, I analyzed the results even more carefully, to determine what went wrong, where I failed, and how I could have done something differently to resolve the problems I encountered. You can learn from my mistakes!

As I said earlier, none of this is brain surgery, but until you have experienced a local campaign first-hand, you won't ever know this stuff. When the snow is blowing in your face, when your spouse is questioning your sanity, when you can't remember what day it is, and your eyelids hurt, this book can help pull you through. When you are wearing out shoe leather faster than you can afford shoes; when you find yourself speaking to almost empty community halls; and when your trying to find a few more campaign donations, this book will give you strength to continue. I invite you to walk where Denny Hastert and I have walked. Let me share with you my campaign successes and failures. You can learn from me and will probably improve upon the advice that is offered.

Running for public office and serving my fellow citizens has been a wonderful experience that is worth every moment of time I put into it. Being a representative in your community, in whatever elected capacity, be it school board, planning commission, alderman, or township supervisor, is an honor and a privilege. It will make you feel as if you are truly participating in the democratic process conceived by our forefathers over two hundred years ago. The journey is well worth the effort, and it is an experience that you will not regret. Good luck on this journey!

The Urge To Serve

Before you go out and sign up to be an Alderman, the Mayor, the county Coroner, or a School Board Trustee in your town, you must examine whether you really have the 'urge to serve'. Have you truly considered what is involved in making this commitment to public service? Have you determined what you are truly getting yourself into? Do you really have the stuff your friends and neighbors will need to see in you, to gain their confidence and then represent their interests? These are important questions you should consider before you make the plunge.

If you want to be a leader in your community, you first have to understand what it actually means. Many people have spoken about public leadership, but Robert Greenleaf perhaps stated it best in his book, **"Servant as Leader"**, when he wrote:

> **"The servant—leader is servant first…It begins with the natural feeling that one wants to serve, to serve first. Then conscious choice brings one to aspire to lead. He or she is sharply different from the person who is a leader first, perhaps because of the need to satisfy an unusual power drive or to acquire material possessions. For such it will be a later choice to serve—after leadership is established. The leader—first, and the servant—first, are two extreme types. Between them there are shadings and blends that are part of the infinite variety of human nature."**

> **"The difference manifests itself in the care taken by the servant—first to make sure that other people's highest priority needs are being served. The best test, and difficult to administer, is: Do those served grow as persons; do they, while being served, become healthier, wiser, freer, more autonomous, more likely themselves to become servants? And what is the effect on the least privileged in society; will they benefit, or, at least, will they not be further deprived?"**

Robert Greenleaf's words speak volumes about what should be thought about and considered before someone steps forward to volunteer for public service. You have to explore your own personal motivations, and enunciate your personal and public reasons for wanting to serve. The first step should be to explore what your personal desires are and what is motivating you to step up?

Motivations?

How is it that you have come to this potential challenge in your life? Most people have no desire to take on such responsibilities and would not dream of volunteering to serve their community. I hope you have already given some thought about your urge to serve. It's something you should think about at great length, carefully reviewing all your personal motivations. You should ask yourself, why am I interested in this quest to become a public servant? What are my personal goals? Will they mesh with my family and the community at large? Am I interested in giving something back to society? Am I getting involved because of a specific issue or problem in the community? Is it my only concern or are there other issues of interest as well?

There are many questions that should be explored to define the terms and limits of your potential campaign. You should try to determine these motivations to truly understand why you feel it is so important to take on all these responsibilities. The answers will prepare you for the many questions you will be asked by your spouse, family, friends and neighbors, and once the campaign is rolling, from news reporters and perfect strangers as you ring their doorbells and hand out literature.

One of the most important questions will come from your spouse and it may be phrased "What? Are you nuts!" or "Why would you do this to me and the the family?" While such a question may seem harsh, a candidate's life can be a tremendous imposition on the marriage and family unit, as it will consume valuable time, money, and energy with no guarantee of success. Having a clear, well thought out answer for your spouse is critical for his or her support, and will help formulate the cornerstone of your political advocacy. If your spouse is actually encouraging your candidacy, then you may have your first legitimate vote, as long as you stay on your spouse's side of the issues. (I don't take anything for granted).

After you have your spouse's support, look to your family and close friends for support and additional counsel. Ask them what they think of your quest. Then clearly state your reasons for running for public office. If you can do so these statements will earn you votes every time you state them. People want to believe in someone, and will support a person who can articulate their motivation and positions. You need to have a clear understanding of what is motivating you so that you can address these questions, which will be asked every day of the campaign.

Then as soon as you publicly announce your candidacy, the press and various media outlets in your area will come asking these same questions. Determining your motivations early in the campaign effort can actually work in your favor by helping to obtain favorable publicity, public exposure and support, and even help in gathering political contributions.

If you look at national campaigns, the candidates hit the road after they announce they are running so that these questions can be discussed and people can start lining up to support the candidate. People can also show their support with campaign donations once they are comfortable with what you stand for. Get your motivations straight and articulate them well and you will find supporters and financial backing.

So why are _you_ running? Lets explore some reasons you may be running for public office? You will need to present these reasons to countless other people during the campaign, so you should get it clearly in your head, right from the start. I recommend you sit down with pen and paper and write these thoughts out so they can be carefully crafted into clear concepts and ideas. Once your thoughts are clearly defined, you can build a campaign theme around them. Below are some comments you have probably heard other politicians state when asked these types of questions.

"Public Service is its own Reward"

Many a politician has been heard to say 'public service is its own best own reward'. While this may ultimately be true, if you say such a thing, people will just stare at you blankly. Plus, you will have a hard time explaining just what you really mean when asked to elaborate. And the press will ask you because it is their job to do so. Trust me when I say that after you have been elected and have been serving for a while, you will understand what this public service cliché really means. And believe it or not, the statement is very true! Public service is it's own reward. It has been for me. It is a great chance to give something back to your community.

I have tremendously enjoyed the process of getting elected and representing people's interests in managing my community, and in making decisions that will impact my family, home and neighborhood. I like being able to shape what kind of values my community will have, and how the town will grow and prosper. I like having an impact on where development projects will be sited, where commercial businesses and retail stores will be located, and what types of industry and commerce should be encouraged in town.

I like the constant challenges found in a developing community and being an elected official allows me to shape the policies. I still get a rush every time I say the Pledge of Allegiance at the beginning of a Village Board Meeting because I am actively participating in the democratic process of self-government. I embrace this citizen interaction, even when people are upset about an issue, because I remind myself that they felt strongly enough to come out and be heard. I enjoy dealing with safety and quality of life issues, participating in village personnel matters and in determining how the day-to-day business of running a public corporation unfolds. Public service truly is its own reward!

"There's good money to be made"

At the national level perhaps this could be true, especially if the politician gets a great book deal like Bill Clinton did recently, but at the local level you are not going to get rich! In many jurisdictions, there is little or no pay at all. School boards traditionally work without pay and they often put in hundreds of hours a year. And many village boards and councils are only paid small honorariums that rarely even cover your expenses as an elected official. And there are expenses that you will incur. You will find yourself driving all over the community to visit development sites, to examine intersections for a sign or light, or to attend a meeting or hearing. If you do your job right the small amount of salary may not even cover automobile expenses. (But you can deduct such expenses on your taxes.)

Being active in local affairs can be rewarding in many other ways. It's a wonderful opportunity to meet your neighbors, to make interesting and valuable contacts, to develop lasting relationships, and learn how to improve your community. Being a local politician can also help in your business career by giving you more self-confidence and visibility around town. Getting elected allows you to actually participate in the process of making your town a better place to live and raise a family. That can be very rewarding all by itself.

Most local elected positions are part-time, especially in smaller towns and villages. The so-called official time commitment may be just a few hours a week for the Council meetings, but the unofficial commitment is what you personally decide to put into the effort. You must determine how willing you are to take phone calls and e-mails, represent citizen interests, attend extra meetings, visit community sites, attend neighborhood events, and become involved in whatever comes before the Board.

Over the years, I have earned as little as $500 a year and as much as $5,500 as a local public official. I haven't gotten rich being a public servant, so it obviously isn't my motivation for getting involved. It must be something else. You will often see people who have flexible career jobs take on local political positions because they can fit the government service into their busy career schedules. People like attorneys, real estate salespeople, and homemakers have greater flexibility to juggle their jobs and political endeavors. For the most part, suffice it to say you can't live on local politicians pay. The pay, if there is any at all, is not a motivator, especially when you factor in the time and commitment you will put into the job to represent your constituents. So we know it's not the money!

"I'm mad as hell, and I'm not going to take this anymore."

Remember that infamous line Peter Finch yelled out the studio window in the movie "Network" in 1976? It may have been the best line in the whole movie. Are you running for political office because you are angry? Have taxes continued to rise to the point you feel there is 'taxation without representation'? Do you think you can resolve a specific problem better than the current politicians who ignore the issue altogether?

Any of these questions could be motivators to validate your decision to jump into the fray. But, here I would offer some caution. If it is just a single issue or problem that is motivating you, you should probably step back and re-examine your feelings some more. You want to make sure you are not a "one issue" candidate. Pressing one or even two issues may get you elected, but what if after they are then resolved in the first year and now you have to serve for three more years. Will you lose interest in all the other daily concerns and problems in your community? The citizens who elected you to represent their interests will not appreciate a singular focus, and they will hold you to an invisible election contract to represent all their future interests.

Be certain that your desire to become involved goes deeper than any one issue, because becoming a local elected official will expose you to all sorts of other important issues for years to come. You will need to be concerned about annual budgets, zoning issues, garbage collection, multiple levels of taxes, street maintenance, water and sewer lines, referendums, restrictive covenants, unhappy citizens, and labor issues. All these concerns go with the job and you have to have a sincere desire to deal with them or you will be very unhappy once elected for a two year or four year term!

You will need to be interested in how the community spends it's tax dollars, how to fund police and fire safety issues while at the same time funding parks and recreation. You need to understand personnel development because municipal employees and their benefit programs account for more than half of most municipal budgets. You will have to represent the community from a big picture standpoint, while at the same time caring about individual needs for a neighborhood stop sign or a school district special needs class. You must care about all sorts of community concerns, not just that one issue that got you angry in the first place.

Single Interest Motivation

Single-issue motivation can be dangerous for both you and the community. If there is only one issue that is exciting you it may be better to pour your energies into supporting that one issue as an activist, or supporting other candidates that feel as you do. You may get your satisfaction without the considerable effort you would have to put into a campaign. And your community will be better off in the long run.

You must explore your motivations and desires? What is driving you to serve the public's needs? Have you been involved in community affairs? Have you volunteered your time to serve on a commission or task force? Are you active in your church, or volunteering at your children's school? Have you chosen to voluntarily attend village meetings to know what is going on? If so, you have already invested in your community and may want to increase that commitment. This is the right kind of self-motivation.

You should also talk about this with family and friends to get their insights into these matters and to test their support level. You may find them trying to talk you out of getting involved and that will become a good gauge of your desire to wade into this commitment. At the same time you may win them over and they become the nucleus of a support group necessary for any good campaign. Explore these questions before going public and you will be well on your way to building a solid campaign.

My Motivations

My motivation in local politics dates back to the sixties. As a kid I was exposed to the activism of my parents working on local circuit court judge campaigns. I remember the excitement of being involved in something I was studying in school. It made my study of civics seem very real. My parents helped to campaign with a car top carrier sign on the family station wagon. We helped distribute yard signs all over the community. I can still remember watching people go into the polling place from my vantage point in the schoolyard across the street.

After the 1960 election, my father was encouraged by friends to run for a local aldermanic position challenging a well entrenched incumbent. As an 11-year old, I got my first real exposure to the elective process and gained valuable experience in campaigning. I helped my Dad campaign door-to-door, handing out litera-ture, making yard signs and car-top carriers and going to public hearings and council meetings. I was hooked on the excitement that goes with a campaign. Dad's experiences had a lot to do with my desire to get involved.

In High School I was involved in student government all four years. I was never Class President but I served in a number of leadership positions elected by the class. While the school campaigning was different than in a public election, I was able to apply many of the same principles I had learned as a campaign worker for my father. Running for Class Board, I quickly learned it wasn't the end of the world to have to make a speech. It was a challenge, but doing so helped me beat down all those public speaking fears at an early age. I also learned some marketing skills by selling my leadership capabilities to fellow students. Many of these self-taught skills came back to me in later elections and I was glad I had learned them a long time ago.

In college I ran for a variety of positions in student government. I also became a political science major to further understand the whole democratic process and to explore whether I might find some future in government service. I even volun-teered to work as a county worker in the 1972 McGovern Presidential Campaign. McGovern lost all over the country but my County went for him. I was hooked and enjoyed the experience of getting involved!

A few years later, I got married, bought my first home, and received my first property tax bill. I was shocked to find that all sorts of governmental units had their hands in my very shallow pockets. They were taking my hard earned dollars as taxes for local government, schools, libraries, and a host of other taxing districts, plus federal income taxes and on and on. I felt that I didn't have much of a say in how my money was being spent.

So I started thinking about getting involved to try to minimize the tax bite they were taking from me, and my family. I'm sure we have all been there, but I actually wanted to do something about it. So at the relatively young age of 27, in my first home, in a new community, I decided to run for a local aldermanic seat to right all the perceived tax wrongs that were confronting me. I filled out the papers, made up a brochure, rang some doorbells, and promptly lost in the primary just a month later. I pulled less than one hundred votes from close friends and a few neighbors! It was a very quick baptism by fire and it was over before it really got started. But that didn't really bother me because I had gotten into the battle and had my first taste of politics.

I learned some valuable lessons in that first naïve effort and my motivation to get involved became even stronger. After the election, I sought some other way to get involved in my community. I decided to call the Mayor of our town, and he actually took the call because he was aware that I had run for office. He invited me to come in and we talked about my very short campaign experience. He asked me what my motivation had been. (See, that motivation question is important).

I explained my past political involvements as a kid, my Dad's past campaign effort, school activities, and related how I had always had an interest in government. And then I stated that as a new homeowner in the community, I wanted to understand why every taxing district in the world had their hands in my pocket. I wanted to get actively involved. That must have been the right comment because the Mayor asked if I would be interested in serving on the Board of Zoning Appeals. He said it would give me a chance to see government at work, and this type of exposure would help me to understand the many issues the community faced. I immediately said yes and was off to the races.

Becoming a Public Servant

Serving on the Board of Zoning Appeals for five years allowed me to see local government from the inside out. I began to more clearly understand how local government functioned and served the public's best interests by creating order, safety and service. From my vantage point on Zoning, I was also able to observe other government department functions and began to truly understand and participate in the process of governing. I was hooked and this appointed position became the springboard for my second local elective campaign.

Two years later, I entered my second campaign for alderman in a city of 65,000 citizens. I now had a clearer understanding of what needed to be done to accomplish my goals. I was more organized, had reviewed potential issues and created a plan for the campaign. It was an exciting race over a five-month period, against a well-entrenched incumbent. He had held the office for many years and knew everyone in town. Over four thousand votes were cast in the aldermanic district, one of 16 districts. The election went well but I still came up a bit short, a total of 32 votes separated me from the win. I even went through the process of a recount because there were numerous absentee ballots and only seventeen miscounted votes would have swung the result the other way. But in the end, no votes changed hands and I lost for the second time. I had climbed the mountain only to meet defeat again. But in the process of losing I had learned some additional valuable lessons, about myself, and getting elected.

A couple years later, (still on the Zoning Board), I moved my family to a larger home in the same city, and another aldermanic seat came up for election. So I signed up to give it another try and analyzed all my accumulated knowledge of what had failed in the past campaign. I not only won that election, but handily beat another strong incumbent with very solid vote totals. I attributed the win to developing a sound campaign strategy and paying attention to all the details of the elective process.

A good number of years later after serving my four-year term of office, my career work in trade association management took me to the State of Illinois. With the kids growing up, I didn't have the time to run for office, but I helped out in some friends' campaigns for local office, utilizing the election principles I had !earned over the years. I even had a chance to refine some of the techniques I had found successful in the past. All the candidates I helped were victorious. It was almost as much fun as being the candidate. But not quite!

Then in 1998, with the kids all away at college, my spouse and I decided to build a new house in Sugar Grove, a far western suburb outside of Chicago. It was a quiet little village on the edge of the metropolitan circle where a building boom was developing. The village was becoming a fast growing bedroom community with population numbers tripling as new neighborhood developments sprouted all over town. The town was almost like a blank canvas that needed the attentions of a knowledgeable land planner to make sense out of all the development pressure. I became interested in participating in the process of designing this community's build-out, and started investigating what the political scene was all about. I visited the library for some background, attended a few Village Board meetings and asked my neighbors what they thought the issues were.

I thought I now had the time to get involved again and decided to run for one of three Village Trustee spots that were up for re-election. Only two incumbents and another first-time applicant had thus far applied for the three spots, when I threw my hat in the race. Up until that point all three would have been automatically elected, but when my nomination papers were filed it became a competitive elective contest.

As a new resident in the community, I was pretty much overlooked as a viable candidate by the other incumbents. But that was fine with me because I was able to set up an entire political structure under the radar screen and mount a textbook campaign to win one of the seats. I just went about my business and used my accumulated knowledge of past campaigns to organize my time, effectively use my limited personal resources and identify where the voters were located. I was also willing to wear out some shoe leather and that made all the difference in this election! My opponents were initially not out ringing doorbells. I was and quickly realized that the public wasn't used to seeing someone actually come to their homes, they weren't used to having a candidate introduce himself, and thus they remembered me when they went into the election booth.

Even though I was new to the community and virtually unknown, I did win, receiving the most votes of all of the candidates running. I attribute that success to knowing what to do, and how to turn out the vote. I didn't have the luxury of knowing many people, but I did understand how to meet and reach out to them. And that's what this book is all about: being an effective campaigner and getting elected. So lets get you started.

Getting Started

"I will study and get ready, and perhaps my chance will come."
—Abraham Lincoln

It's time to stop promising what will be shared, and actually share some of the finer points of "Getting Elected". You won't win an election just thinking about it, so let's get busy and get the blood pumping. First off, you need to visit your village, city, or county clerk and advise them you are interested in taking out nomination papers for an elective position. A phone call to your local clerk will tell you at what level you need to start your quest. Make sure you get a complete set of rules, ordinances and specific timelines for all the filing requirements. Many a campaign has been tripped up because candidates started too late, missed filing deadlines, or didn't know all the requirements, rules and regulations in the elective process.

Then seek out the village clerk and introduce yourself. Better yet try to make friends with this person from the moment you walk up to the counter. Smile and be friendly, because they can be a big help in getting the ball rolling. These public officials will have all the initial information you will need to know. The secret is to ask for their help.

The clerk will be able to share all the necessary information about the election with you. When asking for nomination papers, a set of state laws will govern the process, plus local ordinances and other requirements that will come into play, and you need to pay attention to all these details. It is also advisable to have an attorney friend assist you in filling out the necessary papers correctly. Often there are documents like the "Statement of Economic Interest" with wording that can be vague or difficult to understand. The clerk cannot advise you in these situations, so if you are unsure, consult an attorney.

A good clerk will have all the documents already made up into a comprehensive packet of information and he or she will advise that all the information is also available with the State Election Board or Commission. This information is intended to provide candidates with the basic information they will need for the correct filing of nomination papers. Failing to follow these rules as they are spelled out can negate the validity of the filing papers thereby preventing you from ever making it to the starting gate.

This information is critical to a good first effort to get the ball rolling. Don't be afraid to ask questions. Remember if you get elected you may become one of their bosses and they already know that so they will be helpful, if you ask.

Assembling a Campaign Committee

Putting a campaign team together is the next most important thing you should think about. This effort is important because it builds the nucleus of a committed team effort, allowing you to focus your energies where they belong, on issue development and the public relations exposure needed to win. If you have a dynamic, active group of dedicated workers willing to handle day-to-day tasks you will get a lot more accomplished and not lose the momentum that is needed to win. So who should be on this important team?

The first person you should recruit is the person that talked you into becoming a candidate. It may be a neighbor, your parents, or your spouse, but they should be at your right hand from the very start. Be aware that this initial person may not be able to officially join your team if they are one of the current politico's who has recruited you to run. Officially they may need to stay neutral, but behind the scenes, they can assist in garnering support, making suggestions, pointing you towards support and dollars and helping as a silent partner. If you have someone like this consider yourself lucky and avail yourself of the talent as much as you can without drawing attention to the person.

The other critical Executive Team member must be your spouse. You need his or her moral support more than anyone else, because they will always be there for you and sometimes they will offer a more objective view on a subject than you can see for yourself. Your pillow talk can be frank and honest discussion that can help direct the campaign. Plus, you don't want people to ask why your spouse isn't supporting the candidate. Even Hillary Clinton never stopped supporting Bill through all his meanderings, and if anyone had a good reason to cut and run, she did!

After that, I encourage you to round out your team based upon what they can bring to the table. Your CPA accounting friend is the one to ask to coordinate finances. They can cut through all the state finance law like it was butter and then you don't have to worry about it other than meeting deadlines and signing reports. If you have a neighbor or friend who has some special talent or business capability, ask them if they would take a position. The advertising executive might enjoy utilizing his business talents in getting you elected. Or someone who is a great writer might be able to handle press releases, brochure language, or speeches that you will need to write.

Your neighbor the carpenter, or the guy with a pick-up truck would be the perfect person to coordinate signage, helping to build them, distribute them, and keeping them up and visible for the duration of the campaign. Other special jobs to fill should be sign helpers to put out your signs and keep them upright through all kinds of weather. Wind, rain, snow, and malicious kids of all ages are your enemy. This alone could be a major category of help depending on the size of the precinct or district.

You should also think about finding writers, political advisors and observers, judges and poll watchers, drivers to get people to the polls, especially the elderly, literature drop coordinators, coffee coordinators, and an advertising and public relations manager.

If you have a large retail area in your district, think about identifying a key businessperson from that area, or someone from the Chamber of Commerce who would act as the retail commercial business coordinator. This person would know how to relate to the businesses and could more readily identify issues they will be concerned about. This person could also help develop answers to business questions that may come up during the course of the campaign.

The same is true if you have a largely working class constituency made up of union workers. Try to identify friends and neighbors who understand these interests and could help you gain credibility with union voters. By knowing whom your constituents are, you can find like people to assist your campaign committee.

Consider having a youth liaison and elderly interests represented on this committee if your constituency has such elements. You want to have diverse, district wide support and understand group and economic issues from the people's standpoint. That's why a representative committee is so important to getting ahead. If the district has many distinct neighborhoods, recruit someone from every area, creating area coordinators that can build mini power bases out of their home with friends and neighbors. If you have a couple of active moms that are involved in school activities, you might ask them to coordinate the political coffee's that will be scheduled. First, they know everyone and their brother, and they can set up a diversified schedule for these types of exposure events where you can meet people and tell them what you are all about. These individuals can also head up brochure distribution efforts and will be able to plug into the PTA or soccer moms network on the days you need people to go door to door.

Think of every potential activity or process you would like to accomplish in the campaign effort and then identify a person who would be a good fit to assist with that job or activity. Keep in mind that you don't have to ask all these people yourself. This is where a good campaign chair becomes invaluable. As the team develops, more activities can be identified, fleshed out and assigned to interested parties.

Besides campaign activities, it also a good idea to line up a couple of good thinkers and strategists, people who will advise you on issue development, help you formulate responses to inquiries and act as mentors to give you objective observations. They can help you prepare solid campaign literature, write speeches that make sense and keep an eye on the big picture because it is easy to get lost in the minutia of a campaign.

Once you have this diversified Campaign Committee identified, bring them together at your house for a kick-off meeting. Put out a nice spread of refreshments (this is a legitimate expense) and make them feel comfortable. Allow everyone to mingle and get to know one another before any official call to order is made. Ideally, you will know most of these individuals and you should informally be introducing people to one another, acting as the nucleus of this group. You want them to feel comfortable so they will feel as if they are a part of the team.

Once everyone is assembled, call the meeting to order and then try to introduce everyone to one another more formally. Make each of these new committee members feel as if they are an important part of the campaign staff and introduce them to the group by saying things like "Sean is a great friend and, as a CPA, has offered to handle campaign finance", or "Marie is my next door neighbor and is very active in the PTA, she will coordinate all the neighborhood literature deliveries". Make all these guests feel good about being there by recognizing them. Tell them they are important to the whole equation, because they are, and they will work hard to get you a victory.

Then you start laying out the campaign, the finance needs, the timelines required, and ask them to guide you through the whole process. You will be surprised how they will rise to the occasion and assist you on your quest.

Make an Organization Chart

Build yourself a good Organization Chart and place everyone on the Campaign Committee somewhere on the chart. You want to show how everyone is involved so that everyone's job is important. Buy some large card stock and create an elaborate pyramidal organization chart that can be put in front of the room. This way everyone can see how you envision the committee functioning, and how important everyone is to the tasks at hand. In fact, put yourself on the bottom of the chart in an inverse pyramid so that people see how important they are in relation to the candidate. This organization chart should also have phone numbers and e-mail addresses in a kind of phone tree format so that participants can communicate with one another as a team.

Next, hand out a detailed agenda of what you hope to accomplish. It should offer a clear picture of the effort to be mounted. You should also distribute a detailed timeline that shows every planned activity up through election day. This will show when you see your signs going up, when the literature drop is scheduled, when the mailings will be sent, when the coffees are planned, and when the public debates or candidate meetings are scheduled. In this manner everyone can see and identify how they fit into the schedule and plan for it.

Everyone assigned a task should have been talked to beforehand. Do not surprise anyone with your announcements about assignments, as that may not be received well. Have it all pre-arranged with one-on-one conversations ahead of time. Then when you run down the list let everyone know how important each of these assignments are. Build everyone up a bit and they will rise to the occasion and do a better job than you expect.

This is also a great time to start collecting some of the campaign fund. Suggest that your Finance Chair quietly, but publicly, offers to write out a $25 or $50 dollar donation to the campaign. Nothing else needs to be said and many of these folks will want to contribute themselves. Never allow this amount to be too high, as then others may feel pressured and resist following suit.

You will be amazed at the ingenuity and resourcefulness of your Campaign Committee. Over the years, I have learned all sorts of things from them and have been a much better candidate because of their insights. They have offered great counsel, told me when I was wrong on an issue, and when I was making a big mistake. Once assembled you will want to keep these campaign committees together to act as a guidance team, offering insights and interpretations on the issues you will have to deal with once elected. Count on your Campaign Committee and they won't let you down. It can be a fun and rewarding experience for them and you and you will gain stronger friendships out of the relationships win or lose.

Issues Development

"If you have an important point to make, don't try to be subtle or clever. Use a pile driver. Hit the point once. Then come back and hit it again. Then hit it a third time—a tremendous whack."

—Sir Winston Churchill

If you have already brought together a good Campaign Committee, these individuals should be asked to examine what the issues will be. A good committee can help you determine what your position should be on a variety of issues. Having a well thought out position on every question can earn you votes. Stammering or saying you don't know will only hurt your efforts to earn voter support. Use your committee to explore issues and prepare comments on all the potential issues that could come up.

These will include your position on street improvements, and garbage pickup, school issues and public employment contracts. What about taxes? This is always a loaded question, because the public rarely understands the complexities of how tax dollars get split among many taxing authorities. Whole chapters could be written on this subject alone, but suffice it to say you should seek out information on how the taxes are broken down and distributed to taxing bodies, so you can offer answers. They may not like what you will tell them but it is important that you give them good information and show them you are on top of the subject.

You should look for a local government pie chart graphic that is usually available from the village. It will show how the tax dollar gets divided up between various taxing authorities. Usually this is a chart attached to the Village or city annual budget. If you can't get such a chart already made up, gather the necessary information and using a computer make one for yourself. You will find the pie chart an invaluable tool to share with voters because taxes are misunderstood across the board. Usually the bulk of the property tax dollar goes to the school district, and only small portion flow to the other government bodies. If you are not running for a school district seat, it is important that you make the distinction to separate yourself from their frustration. If you are the school district you should tell them why the tax assessment is so important.

You should copy this pie chart and carry it with you to every event, and when you go door-to-door. Think of it as a tax deflector because it allows you to defend your candidacy from all the people who think you are to blame for all their tax burdens in the world. A good tax burden pie chart will show them that you are not the problem, but could be a partial solution if elected. All of a sudden they are willing to listen to what you have to say and you can hopefully count on another vote.

Talking about taxes, you should understand who each of the taxing authorities are and what portion they receive. It will assist you in talking about these minefield subjects. If you don't have a good grasp of taxes or the community budget, go back and see your best friend, the village clerk, and ask what information can be reviewed to become an expert. Get a copy of the budget or at least review it and pull the large numbers and facts. It is valuable information that shows you where all the money comes from and more importantly, where it all goes.

Don't worry about not understanding all the individual lines of the budget, you can ask questions of the existing elected officials and have your accounting chairman break it down for you. A lot of the numbers and sub-categories are just repetitive line items showing how the maintenance department buys its supplies, or how the street repair process is budgeted for the year. But you should become familiar with the overall budget, the various revenue sources, what the major expenditures are and how the money is utilized to provide basic government services. You will find that police and fire protection, village personnel, and basic infrastructure, like streets, water, and sewage control chew up most of the budget.

Have a CPA friend analyze the budget for you, and give you a crash course on where all the money comes from and where it all goes. You will be shocked and impressed by the diversification of categories and the amount of financial control that is exhibited. All of this budget and cost information will give you a better understanding of issues that may come into play in the election. People will often say 'show me the money ', and then I always say 'follow the money' and try to understand what all the tax dollars mean and where do they go.

For additional issues development start monitoring the local newspaper to identify existing issues and potential new ones. Local reporters make a good faith effort to stay on top of all activities within the governmental unit and can give you some great insight into what is developing as an issue.

Don't be afraid to talk with a reporter, but be aware that they have a job to do reporting the news and you may quickly become a part of that news. If you don't want to be quoted or identified as a source on an issue, clearly tell the person that your conversation is off the record at the start of the conversation. A good reporter will honor your request from an ethical standpoint. They also want to work with you in the future and maintain that trust. A bad reporter may abuse the privilege you are extending to him, but it will only happen once. I rarely would talk about anything confidential as I have found you can't trust the people to hold the confidence. If it is confidential, I try very hard to keep it that way at least from my standpoint.

I would encourage you to monitor these newspapers for months in advance to pick up trends and see how the existing elected officials handle various issues. Do the officials tend to vote together or is there dissention in the ranks. If you are running against an incumbent you need to closely monitor voting habits and where your opponent stands on issues.

You should start charting performance by issue and type so that you can determine the fiscal conservancy of your opponent. You can get copies of voting records from the village clerk as the minutes of the council meetings are public record. You should be able to determine how liberal or conservative the incumbent is and then determine how you will challenge those positions.

You should also start attending the local governmental meetings and also attend other meetings that directly relate. That may mean blocking out every Tuesday night for the Council, and once a month on Wednesday evenings for the Plan Commission. In this manner you will begin to understand how things work and you will get a feel for the issues.

You should also seek to identify potential issues by attending various meetings of the home and school board, neighborhood watch, the Police and Fire Commission, and perhaps even the neighboring community town meeting. Being seen at these events may even earn a few votes as your zeal will be noticed when citizens go into the voting booth. Ask someone what they think about an issue to help formulate your position. People will be very willing to share their thoughts and you will gain greater insight into all sorts of issues.

Other candidates and current officeholders can also help you on current issues. They can be very sharing, unless they are in your opponent's camp. Then you should be on guard in what you say and how you position yourself, as it most likely will get back to the other guy. But don't shy away from the conversation. It will show your opponent you are actively engaged turning up at all sorts of events and asking lots of questions. You can intimidate your opponent without even trying.

I have found that it is best to create a filing system on all the major issues and gather materials that will assist you in understanding what they are all about. These files should be shared with your Campaign Committee to help you formulate positions, answer questions and to create speeches. File materials can come from legal documents, articles, candidate brochures, notes from meetings and other forms of documentation. I would also suggest visiting your local library to catch up on community reading, council summaries and developing issues that may become questions.

Curve Ball Issues

There is another campaign concern you should be aware of. You will occasionally get questions about issues that will come at you from left field, or outer space, issues that will not be relevant to the local government unit you are running for. These are curve ball issues and they are very hard to hit.

People at the local level will ask for your opinions on abortion, the war in the Middle East, your concern for global warming, and people wearing animal fur. While these are legitimate issues they are usually way outside the sphere of the local community issues. Always keep in mind that anything you might personally feel about these issues, will not be a factor because they have nothing to do with local government. If you offer a personal view on these global issues you may earn a vote, but you may also lose a vote. It is often better to steer clear of why we shouldn't allow oil exploration in Alaska, because your local community will not have an impact on the issue.

There is no good answer or safe way to be responsive to these inquirers because no matter what you say, you will invariably find yourself on the wrong side of the issue. You will probably anger the questioner, or the next guy he or she talks to, and possibly lose a vote over a non-issue that you could not possibly make a political difference on. I have seen elected officials try to solve world problems at village meetings and no one was satisfied with what they had to say. It's a no-win situation and your best way to deal with such questions is to stay out of it.

An exception to this general rule would be when a controversial issue does directly relate to a local concern. As an example, if the question is about abortion and an abortion clinic is actively applying for a local zoning variance to build a clinic in your town, then it may become an issue you will have to take a position on. In such cases, you probably would want to keep relating the issue to the zoning ordinances and whether they qualify just as other businesses would under the law. It won't win you these particular voters endorsement because they are tying the zoning to a much larger political and ethical issue, but you should try to keep the two separate if possible. In these situations, you can also suggest inquirers contact the more appropriate levels of government such as the Governor, or their Senator to deal with these concerns, and then move on.

Venturing into these areas will usually draw an even bigger crowd, including the press, which can expand the exposure and the problem for you personally. Then such questions can become personal challenges to your campaign and expose you to bad publicity. It's a situation that you cannot win, no matter what position you may take.

Party Affiliation

Another question that comes up quite regularly is your political party affiliation. You can usually presume that the person asking is active in one party or another, and wants to know where you stand. In my experience the person asking the question is always from the other party, regardless of what your affiliation may be. Thus, you have another loaded question that will cause you to possibly lose a vote even before they know anything about you.

In all of my local political campaigns the elective races have always been non-partisan, meaning no party affiliation is declared, nor necessary for the office being sought. When you advise the questioner that it is a non-partisan election, they are often satisfied and let it go. But some people still want to know what your underlying political philosophy is because it will help them understand how you approach government and how you might vote on issues. With such a question you have to decide what you want to tell them. If you have done your homework, you will know what the community leanings are and can gauge how inflammatory your party affiliation response will be.

If your election is run along partisan lines you will have to declare your party status or state that you are running as an independent. If it is a partisan election there will also be rules that the party enforces and there will be procedures for primary voting and getting on the ballot. Once you have declared your party status, the party will advise you what the rules of engagement are, what you can do as a candidate, and how you will run your campaign. The good news is that they may also be willing to help with some money or in-kind donations, and offer foot soldiers to help distribute brochures. But don't count on it because they are usually spread pretty thin. Declaring a party affiliation can work to your benefit if you are in a so-called red or blue area of the state and that is your party. But it can just about kill you if you're from the other party.

So you may want to actually declare you are an independent to defeat all the party affiliation baggage that you would otherwise have to carry. That is a great subject for your kitchen cabinet to discuss. Years ago, you couldn't win if you weren't affiliated with a certain party in certain areas. Chicago Democrats comes to mind although that isn't as true anymore as people have become sophisticated enough to not just vote party lines. Today they often look at candidates and what they stand for and determine their vote based on issues.

In many local elections, party affiliation is not a factor and you run as non-partisan candidates. In these situations it may be to your advantage to not lean towards any party as that could prevent some people from voting for you, or just the opposite, it might help to affiliate with a party even though it is a non-partisan election. That's another discussion you should have with your advisors.

Aligning with a particular party may have financial advantages, as that party may have funding resources available to persons who espouse party beliefs. Again it is something you must check out and discuss with advisors. Your county chairmen in both parties can offer advice on the benefits of formally affiliating in a particular party.

The bottom line is you will be asked about your affiliation by the press, various organizations, other candidates and the general public. Think about what your answer will be ahead of time so it comes out coherently and you are not stumbling. In non-partisan elections, you may be best served by simply stating it is a non-partisan election, and as such no party affiliation is involved. Depending on the situation and the person, you may care to volunteer a personal preference if you think it could make someone more comfortable, but that is often a crap shoot and you alienate as many people as you embrace.

Endorsements

Once you have decided to run you should also consider whether or not there are key people, or groups in the community that might consider endorsing you for office. Some candidates swear by endorsements while other think they are highly overrated. Overall, endorsements from individuals and groups can be useful as long as you don't have to give much away to earn them. If you are asked for favors, or the promise of a future vote, should you be elected, the endorsements are not worth the price, but if they are unencumbered, an endorsement can have a positive effect on people. I would temper that statement by saying an endorsement from one group might also be a major turnoff to another organization. A good example would be an endorsement by a radical group might mean the police union will not support you. In a situation like this you have to balance the benefits against the down side to see if seeking the endorsement is worth the related aggravation and loss of support from another sector.

An endorsement can be a great vote generator if it is the right people or groups making the endorsements. With all potential endorsements you want to check out who is making the offer. You don't want the local Mafia Don to give you an endorsement even if he is your great uncle. In a case like that you should ask Guido to quietly support you, perhaps make a small donation, (and small is the operative word as someone else can look at your financial records), and ask him to talk to his other family members about also voting for you. Leave it at that because a greater endorsement from him could actually hurt you more than help.

On the flip side, your local priest or Rabbi, the school principal, existing politicians, or the Mayor would all be great endorsements to have supporting you and in your campaign literature. But you will often find these individuals will want to stay neutral in the campaign because they don't want to alienate anyone. Remember they will also have to work with your opponent if you lose. It's their job to stay above campaign politics, especially if they are not running.

You can get around the politician endorsement issue by instead having your photograph taken with the person. While there is no overt endorsement, there is an unofficial endorsement presumed by those who would view the picture. That is why you will see politicians crowd around the President or Governor as a Bill is signed into law. There is an implied bond in the photo. At the same time, the President carefully determines whom he wants in those pictures because he understands there is an implied endorsement and the public can and will make a connection based on such a photograph.

If you are looking to encourage endorsements look for people who know lots of other people, as they will promote your candidacy to their friends, neighbors and fellow employees. The CEO of the major employer in town might be a good prospect if you would like to get the attention of his employees, presuming they value his judgment of character. If they dislike the CEO his sponsorship would have a negative effect with the employees. Thus you have to weigh the pros and cons of each potential endorsement. This process is a good job for your Kitchen Cabinet as they can sample sentiment before any endorsement is sought or given.

The priests or ministers at the local churches are usually influential in their religious community and may be willing to endorse your candidacy once it is known what you stand for. The President of the PTA knows everyone and would be an important endorsement if you could get it. Then you could go a step further and ask that a flyer be sent to all the parents encouraging their support. The head of your village employee union would also be a good person to ask for an endorsement. He or she will want to know that you intend to be a friend of the workingman, specifically the employees of the community. You have to weigh what that endorsement will actually cost once you are voting on salary, personnel, and employee arbitration issues.

Concerning individual endorsements, don't be afraid to ask people to talk you up to their friends and neighbors. That is how the campaign spreads and how you build an ever-increasing drum beat of interest that culminates on Election Day.

If you can line up a good number of endorsements, you may want to create an advertisement simply saying:

"The Citizens of (Town) Proudly Support the Candidacy of (name)", and then list each person in small type. You can even turn this into a self paid advertisement by asking those signing to donate $10 to defray the costs of the ad. The ad should be run in the local newspaper paper the weekend before the Primary or General Election to get the most value out of it. Once you have run such an ad, other people may contact you to join their neighbors in supporting your candidacy. Ask them to help defray the costs (keeping it inexpensive to join in) and you can run the ad again with even more names supporting your election. Such an ad could also be reproduced on paper and distributed as part of your campaign literature.

Nomination Papers
The Official Candidates Petition

Nomination papers are kind of like horse race entry forms. You can't leave the gate without them. The official "Statement of Candidacy" petition must be circulated to the citizenry in your town or district and a certain number of legitimate voters have to sign the papers to get your name on the official ballot for your particular race. All of these matters are governed by state law, election commissions, and local procedures and have been designed to protect people and guide campaigns. This area is very strictly governed by time-tested policies and procedures all based on state election law. You would be surprised at how much hanky-panky has gone on over the last century when it comes to getting people elected and on the ballots. Also, you would be shocked at all the challenges that have occurred over the years to people being placed in nomination.

There are countless court cases that have been brought to challenge the nomination process. Because of these cases, state governments have devised all sorts of laws to make sure that all individuals and parties conform to stated procedures. One almost universal requirement is that signatures on nomination papers must be in ink and affixed there by registered electors who are qualified to vote in the jurisdiction.

A candidate may serve as their own Nomination circulator although they may not sign their own form as a voter, because they are the actual person being nominated. A circulator may not be allowed to sign the same petition or Nominating Form they are actually circulating, but can sign a form being circulated by someone else. It may seem confusing but it is worth sorting out at the front end of the process so you don't run into problems down the road.

In a very recent campaign in an Illinois town, there was a challenge to a candidate's nomination papers because his wife had signed the Nominating Form first as a voter, and later had officially authenticated the numerous documents as a

Notary Public. In Illinois, there was a legal question about whether the notarizer could also sign the paper as a voter. It was determined that the single page that had 20 voter signatures on it including the wife's signature was disallowed. The other papers she had notarized were allowed. The good news was that the candidate had enough signatures so that when that page of twenty signatures was thrown out he still had sufficient signatures to get his name on the ballot.

If political party affiliation is a factor in the race, then you only want qualified electors from that particular party or those who are independent and have not affiliated with a particular political party. In most cases a voter is considered to be a member of a political party if he or she voted in that party's primary election within the preceding year or perhaps longer.

After the Nomination forms and petitions have been circulated the circulator must sign the document attesting that they witnessed each signature being made, and that to the best of the circulators knowledge the signers were qualified to sign, as qualified electors. You will not always know that they are qualified to sign and that is why a number of extra signatures is a good idea.

The number of qualified signatures required on Nomination papers can vary depending on the office being sought, from as little as 10–20 names, to thousands of signatures for larger constituencies. Often the required number is a floating number calculated by determining the total votes cast in a prior election. In Illinois, 5% of that prior election total vote count is the number of signatures required. This percentage will change from state to state so it is worth finding out your target number is. In my most recent local election, 5% meant that only 63 qualified signatures were required on nomination papers to place a candidate on the ballot. Over 90 signatures were turned in just to be safe.

It is critical to know how many voter signatures are required. Always keep that figure in mind because if you are required to turn in 50 names and that's all you actually submit, invariably, some of the people who signed your nomination papers may be ineligible to sign for any number of reasons. Perhaps, because they aren't registered, (often they will sign and not tell you that), or because they didn't advise they live in another jurisdiction.

If 100 signatures are required and that's all you turn in, and then three are disallowed, you would not meet the minimum and your name would not be on the official ballot. You are out of the running before you get started! So pay attention to the minimum number required. A good rule of thumb would be to get at least 10%–20% more than you need to turn in. That way if some names are deemed bad and thrown out, you still meet the minimum. Always err on the high side and that way you don't have to worry.

The Village President in my hometown always tries to get three times the number required. By doing that he feels he may cause some concern with his other challengers who ring the same doorbells and have the residents refuse to sign another nomination because they already signed his. Having extra signatures also negates petition challenges from other candidates, because they know that even if they can identify a number of bad signatures, there are still more than enough to qualify the candidate.

Keep in mind that if you go way over the minimum number of signatures required you won't necessarily endear yourself to the Clerk when you turn in the papers. And remember you want the clerk as your best friend through this whole process. The clerk is required to verify the legitimacy of all the signers, determining that they are registered voters in the local governmental unit, and that the address and signature listed are real and valid. If you turn in hundreds, or thousands of names, theoretically the clerk has to check each one of them to determine they are valid electors. The clerk may not do that once the minimum is truly met, but if any other candidate or political party were to challenge the legitimacy of your nomination papers, the clerk would have to check further. Make a friend out of your clerk by not turning in an excess of names. But be sure to give yourself enough wiggle room! I will offer an even better idea in a future section that allows you to more effectively use the Nominating process.

Statement of Candidacy &
Loyalty Oath

In addition to the Official Candidate's Petition (another name used for Nomination Papers) you may be asked to submit an <u>Official Statement of Candidacy,</u> and perhaps a Loyalty Oath. These documents also become part of the official filing and may need to be notarized as well. If they are required, make sure that you have them filled out and filed correctly by whatever deadline is mandated. The official statement of Candidacy is a form that officially says you are seeking a political office. It means that you are officially in the race.

In a recent U.S. Senate campaign, a candidate from Illinois was forced to step aside for questionable activity in his personal life at a relatively late date, but he did not formally withdraw his Statement of Candidacy. His Party was unable to designate a replacement until the former candidate officially withdrew his name and it caused quite a controversy. Once he was finally persuaded to withdraw, a new candidate was named and submitted papers to officially take over that party's nomination for the Senate. While the paper may not seem important it could be a deal breaker if it is required and not officially filed.

The <u>Loyalty Oath</u> is required in some jurisdictions and simply states that if elected that you will uphold the laws of the land and you will swear loyalty to the office held and the citizens you will represent. The Oath will also state your loyalty to the laws of the federal and state government in addition to the locality. Again, if such papers need to be filed in your election, you cannot pass Go if they are not officially filed. Pay attention to the fine print and meet all the deadline requirements in order to stay in the race.

Statement of Economic Interest

Many states may have requirements for your disclosure of certain financial information that must be made available for public scrutiny. These official forms must be carefully reviewed, perhaps by your attorney or accountant and then filled out correctly.

In Illinois, a <u>Statement of Economic Interest</u> form needs to be filed in the County in which you reside. This form typically asks you to record any business relationships that you have that could come into play if you were elected as a public official, and then had to vote on matters that relate to these interests. The presumption is that the public should have a right to know if you have an economic interest in the street-paving firm that regularly bids on local street repair contracts, because you may have to approve such contracts. Such an interest could be financial or personal, say your brother-in-law is the owner of that paving firm that does business with the city. Or, it could be that the firm you are employed by provides products or services to the community or other branches of local government. These are economic interests that must be exposed for public scrutiny.

While these are obvious relationships that may generate a potential conflict of interest if you are elected to vote on related matters, there are many less obvious ways that a person could use an elected position to influence a government contract. You can read about influence pedaling in the newspapers all the time. It is to your advantage to be honest and list all relationships that your personal or business activities may interact with your local government.

Listing any such relationships will not prevent you from being on the ballot, but will disclose the relationship for public scrutiny. It simply allows the public to be aware that you may have some relationship with a business or person doing business in the community. If ultimately elected, you may feel an obligation to abstain from discussions, or abstain from voting. By listing such relationships and then staying neutral you minimize any impact on a decision, and this will allow you to get around any potential conflict of interest. By listing these potential conflict relationships publicly, you also remove any challenge from an opponent that you are being self-serving and do not have the community's best interests in mind.

In a recent local campaign here in Illinois, one candidate did not bother to file his Statement of Economic Interest (it had to be filed at the County Clerk's office some 10 miles away) and as such did not meet the formal criteria to be placed on the ballot. His campaign ended before it even got started.

In one of my recent campaigns, as the sitting Village Trustee, I had filed an Economic Interest Statement 6 months prior to the start of a campaign, a twice a year requirement for all elected officials. I initially thought this filing would suffice, but upon further inquiry (I asked, just to be sure), I determined the official Economic Statement on file had to be recorded in the current calendar year of the election. My additional investigation and questions allowed me to re-file my Economic Statement in the current year before the deadline. Otherwise I would not have been on the ballot. In another community, this issue forced another candidate off the ballot because he hadn't filed it by the deadline date. Check out all the details and then have someone else double check them.

A Better Nominating Papers Idea

Before, I suggested there may be an even better way to circulate and gather your Statement of Candidacy signatures. While doing this circulation for nominating signatures, you can use your papers quite effectively to line up votes, explore contribution/donation options, and to develop future sign locations all while you are in the early stages of your campaign. Earlier I had said that you shouldn't turn in too many signatures and multiple sheets of nomination papers, because the clerk has to check all the documents you do turn in. While that is true, it is perfectly legal to circulate multiple nomination sheets that people can sign. Just don't turn them all in!

Circulating a Nominating Form is an excellent way to tell people you are running for office. It gives you a legitimate reason to ring a constituent's doorbell, often much earlier than you normally would, and ask them to think of you as a candidate for office. The Nominating Form will clearly state that the signers: "do hereby petition that the person named on the form shall be a candidate." It also states that the signers will be voting for you. This would suggest that every time you gather a signature you are creating a possible vote for yourself and a possible supporter in the actual election.

Nomination Papers can be used as an effective campaign tool to meet and greet people, going door-to-door, or standing in front of businesses where people go to do their errands. Places like the local grocery or hardware store, the local bank or library (most customers will be local people from the neighborhood). It's easy to have the nomination papers on a clipboard and ask for their signature to get on the ballot. Give them a simple handout explaining why your running. It doesn't have to be fancy, as you may not have developed a complete campaign brochure yet, but it could be something stating your motivation (again) and letting them know who you are.

Most people will stop and sign, and then you get a chance to talk about issues, and ask for their support in some way. That could be as simple as putting up a sign in their front yard, or talking to their neighbors. It could even be a way to seek a small contribution if your reason for running is important to them. As an example, presume you are running to protect a parkland open area from development. If you were to stand by an adjacent school, most of the parents dropping off kids would have a vested interest in seeing that land maintained as parkland, and they may want to support your candidacy by signing the papers. They might even ask to help, offer financial support or volunteer to put up a sign in their front yard. All you do is say hello and ask!

Pick the right place and the related issues and you may find people willing to help out. Be creative, if your challenging a school issue, attend the home and school meetings with the nomination papers and pass them around, or better yet have family or friends assist you so <u>you</u> control where those nomination papers are floating.

When there is a neighborhood event or a party, slip the papers in your pocket. My wife doesn't like it when I turn a party into a campaign event, so I try to quietly pass the papers to friends and neighbors, without making a big deal out of it. Friends are usually happy to sign up, sometimes offering to help out with money. Look for opportunities to have your nomination papers signed and you will have no problem getting on the ballot.

Now, if you are successful and do gather hundreds and hundreds of signatures what should you do? You should only turn in about 10-20 % more than you will need to qualify for the ballot and keep the rest for future use. And what would you want all those names for? They are the future mailing lists, sign locations and financial donors of your campaign.

Another thing to do when searching for nomination signatures is to recruit new voters. You will find people willing to sign your Nominating Form that are not even registered. Usually they won't tell you but will readily sign the Form. (Caution: If these non-registered citizens do sign your forms promising to register, don't count them in the required number as they may not actually register and won't be counted) Always have them sign the Nomination Form anyhow, and then give them voter information and encourage them to get registered by directing them to the village or city hall, the library, or the police or fire stations. If you make the effort seamless enough, they will often make the effort and actually get themselves registered. You will have lined up a vote because they appreciated your effort. Carry the voter registration information with you (you can get it from the village clerk) so that when you go to a party or the grocery store you can help people get registered. You won't believe how many people aren't registered until you experience the low voter turnouts. Help your community out by encouraging voter registration.

You can also become a Voter Registrar quite easily if your laws allow it. Even though you may be a candidate or considering it, you can still volunteer as a Registrar helping people to register at a church or some other venue. You can show people you care by posting a table sign that simply says:

"Voter Registration Here—Jane Doe—Registrar—Have I.D. ready."

With all the people you sign up, send a short thank you note and encourage them to vote in the election. Candidates can get lists of newly registered voters, and they are great prospects to court as you begin your campaign.

I live in an area where there are many new subdivisions sprouting up each year and these citizens are new to the community. I will often go door-to-door in these areas asking for nomination support. It gives me first crack at new potential voters. These folks will remember your name when they do vote in their first local election. When I am passing my nomination papers around and I meet someone truly interested in what I'm doing, I will be bolder and ask them if they would allow me to put a sign in their yard, or I will ask them if they would make a $10 or $20 dollar donation to my campaign. The most important thing is to try and create some excitement and exposure in your campaign effort. If you walk up to a person without a plan, you won't convert them. But if you have a compelling reason to approach them, you can make the contact work.

Suffice it to say, I have seen campaigns won and lost with the nomination papers effort alone. Put some thought into how you want to do this initial effort and everything afterwards will be a little bit easier because you will have created some momentum, excitement and visibility. If you are in a larger campaign with multiple signatures required, you will want to expand this effort even more. The clerk can give you a number of official "Nominating Papers", or "Candidate Petitions". Whatever they are called in your jurisdiction, ask and be sure you can copy them, to make multiple copies. But the candidate information and the various fill-in blocks with the names and addresses of who is actually passing the form must be signed in original ink. So copy the forms and then fill in the pertinent general information, like name, office, county, your home address, etc. on each original. But leave the name of the person actually passing the form for you blank until the sheet is distributed to that person. Once it is completely filled in, often with 20–25 signatures, then have them officially sign that they personally passed the document and secured the signatures.

In a large district, you should also make an effort to expand your signature quest outside your immediate neighborhood. By going over to the other side of town, you let more people know about your candidacy, you get some cross town exposure and visibility, and you may put a little fear in your opponents if you are on their side of town. Psychological campaign warfare is an important part of any good campaign.

These additional forms can be distributed to family, friends, neighbors, and your committee members. Have them seek out signatures at the banks, schools, grocery and hardware stores, and gas stations. However, be sure to ask permission first. You don't want to be run off the property! And some chain stores may require corporate approval to stand outside their front door.

The people actually passing your nomination papers must officially sign the form when the 20 or 25 name slots are filled up. They personally attest witnessing the voters have signed the document. You will have some names thrown out because the signers were not registered, or just arrived from Nepal and aren't citizens, but that's ok as long as you have enough signers.

Another thing I do with the lists of people signing is send them a short follow-up letter or postcard thanking them for assisting me and encouraging them to get involved in the campaign. Think of it as a courtesy follow-up and a great way to permanently engrave your name in their minds. It is also a great follow-up opportunity to ask for a sign location, or ask for a small campaign donation. Also, remember to thank all the people who have passed your petitions. It makes them feel as if they have contributed and they will then want to help in some other way. And there are many things that will need to be done.

Sending a short thank you reinforces your name and image, and you may convert them to some more overt campaign activity. I have sometimes listed a half dozen options for getting involved, things like putting up a sign, holding a coffee with neighbors, handing out literature, acting as a campaign judge, or making phone calls before the election. With a little effort you can convert some of these casual signers into campaign workers. Think of the Nomination papers as your first piece of campaign literature because it is getting your name in front of the public and identifying prospect voters.

Filing your Papers

So now that you have these official stacks of papers and names, what do you do with them? Your Nomination papers will have to be notarized when they are turned in. In some communities the village clerk, who will be a Notary, may not want to be the person notarizing the filer's signature, as they will be the official recipients of these same documents. Check ahead of time if they will notarize them for you when you file. If not, have a different Notary Public do it ahead of time.

Often banks and law offices have people with notary capability and only charge nominal fees for their official witness and stamp. You only need to notarize the ones that will be turned in, but remember to turn in 10-20% more than the required number.

I would also suggest you copy all the nomination papers for your personal records because you won't see them again once they are turned in, and they have important voter information on them. You can use them as worksheets to transcribe information to your polling lists that will be used once the campaign is in full swing. Remember these folks promised to vote for you and you want to keep their names and addresses in mind. Once you have copies of all these documents, you have to officially turn them in by a specific date and time.

It is important that you know when the official Filing Date is and the specific time that the filing period opens and closes. In many states that specific filing period will be a narrow window of opportunity for a week, or at most a month. But once the window of filing closes you will not be able to still get in there and file late. You need to know what that ultimate date is and be there with time to spare. There will be a definite final deadline date posted.

The deadline date will be specific. It will usually be at the end of the clerk's office workday, on a particular weekday date at the city or village hall. And if you are five minutes late, you may just be flat out of luck; so don't cut it too close.

Get there on time because the papers have to be officially reviewed and notarized. I would arrive at least an hour before the ultimate deadline and give yourself a bit of a cushion.

Your First Filing Day

The Filing Day is a critical date because it makes you an official candidate. Filing publicly announces your intentions and signals the opening bell for the campaign. This can also be a day to utilize some psychology with your opponents when filing your nomination papers.

If you want to scare off potential candidates, get your nomination papers filled out early in the nominating period, and turn them in as soon as the filing day window opens. On that first day you can show up at the clerk's office ahead of the appointed time and be the first in line. After you officially file the papers, call a press conference, (let the press know you will have a statement for them that morning), or at least issue a press release, stating you are excited about the race and outline what you see as issues. The fact that you have all your ducks in order already could depress other potential candidates who may still be thinking about filing, or still getting their papers together. They may decide not to play catch-up. There is also another reason you may want to file as soon as you can.

Ballot Position

In some communities the order of position on the ballot is determined by when the nomination papers are actually turned in. You must determine the first day official filing date. And you can determine that by asking the clerk. In some past elections, I have gathered my Nomination papers and showed up at city hall as early as 6:00 am to be the first in line to file at 8:00 am.

If your community does allow the first officially filed candidate first position on the ballot, obtaining that spot may be worth a few extra votes. Invariable some voters will turn out on Election Day and won't have a preference in your race. They will often just tick off the top candidate when they don't know who is on the ballot. It happens all the time so first position on the ballot can generate votes.

I encourage you to get up early on that first Filing Day, grab a large cup of strong coffee and a large box of doughnuts (you will see why in a moment), bring a lawn chair for some comfort, a blanket for the morning chill, and camp out next to the front entrance of City Hall. This way you will have a shot at being first in line. But don't be surprised when you arrive and see five other candidates are already in line ahead of you. Don't get frustrated either, there is still a great opportunity waiting.

Walk up and join the line, get out the lawn chair and set up shop. Introduce yourself to the other candidates, offer them a doughnut, and get a conversation going. You may find they are running for other political offices and not against you. You may actually be the first in line for your race. Or you may finally meet all the people that will be challenging you.

Show your confidence and find out as much as you can about your future opponents. It is a great opportunity to listen to comments and size up the opposition to help you formulate campaigning strategies. That's why I always bring a dozen doughnuts with me. Donuts make people comfortable. I'm always amazed at what other candidates will share and talk about if you encourage them. If they casually mention to someone they are going door-to-door, then you know what you have to do to challenge that effort. Be good at listening and you will hear that a candidate is only doing two mailings and leaving the effort at that. That would be useful information, if you can believe them. But it will still be more than you knew a couple hours earlier.

In some communities if multiple candidates all file on the opening day, the community may allow <u>all</u> the candidates present to be filed at the same time, and local policy may allow a lottery to be used for ballot position. By showing up at dawn and being a part of this group, you may get lucky and still win the first position on the ballot. Again, ask the clerk what the policy for ballot position is ahead of time and act accordingly. By the way, being last on the ballot is often better than being in the middle of the pack of candidates because some voters with no preference will choose the last candidate listed.

Concerning filing approaches, I have also seen candidates that have covertly obtained their signatures, waiting until the eleventh hour to show up on the final filing day. This approach may keep opponents guessing whether or not a potential candidate is going to run. In one election three incumbents thought they had the election sewn up for the three seats that were available. At 4:30 pm. on the final filing day, five additional candidates turned papers in. No one even knew they planned on running, and all of a sudden the original three had a real race on their hands. When a large number of candidates are filing, find out if and when there will be a primary election to reduce the number of candidates. If a primary is called for, it will dramatically change your campaign strategy because you may only have a month to make that first early election cut.

There can be a lot of strategy worked into filing and getting a certain ballot position, so you should talk all these things over with your campaign committee and other elected officials to see what they may suggest before acting. You should clearly evaluate and understand all the options, deadlines and the ramifications of your actions, before you have to make a snap decision that could cause problems. That is why I encourage you to build a good campaign team and ask for their opinions and advice whenever you can.

Your First Press Release

During the open filing period, the Clerk may be directed by law to officially advise the press about who has actually filed for a political office. Or they may voluntarily advise the press about candidates actually filing papers. Be aware that once your papers are filed you could immediately start receiving calls from the press asking for comment or asking for background information on you because you are new to the political scene and they don't know a thing about you. This may happen right at Village Hall as you are filing. In some cities the press will be there because they can build a story around the candidates and the coming race. Be prepared to answer their questions, keeping your motivations in mind, because they immediately ask why you decided to run, and where you stand on current issues. While still standing in line, treat this as an opportunity to get some initial exposure for your campaign. If you are caught off guard, politely ask them to call you another specific time (so you can formulate a solid response). You have to presume you will be quoted. You can beg off this one time, but you can't use that excuse too often.

Press inquiries should be considered promotional opportunities not intrusions. It's a great way to introduce yourself to the public who will be asked to vote for you. To really get in front of this situation, prepare an official press release ahead of time and bring it with you to the clerk's office in case any press are hanging around (believe it or not they may be waiting to see who will be filing to do an article listing all the candidates at once). Personally hand out your full press release and introduce yourself. You might get them to print the release verbatim giving you great exposure right off the bat. I would also send or hand-deliver the press release to all the other local newspapers, the radio stations, the television stations etc. In these ways you can use the filing requirements to your advantage.

In many past campaigns, I have prepared complete press releases that said exactly what I wanted them to say with carefully crafted statements. Some times these statements have been almost printed verbatim, giving me excellent early exposure in the campaign. Without such a carefully prepared press release, you are at the mercy of the reporter to interpret what you say.

Your biggest worry should always be that you could be misquoted in a verbal situation. That would do you and your campaign great harm before you even got started. It is much better to hand out the carefully prepared release document that clearly states your positions. It is less likely to be misinterpreted. I learned a long time ago to be careful in what I say and offer to the press to minimize misinterpretation. A good press release can protect you best.

I like to think I have received good press coverage because I prepared good releases worthy of print. I try to make the press release work for me while at the same time meeting the needs of the reporter, the paper or the media outlet that is present and asking for information. As reporters they want to know who, what, where, and when information. Delivering these basics along with carefully constructed quotes that can be picked up word for word makes everyone's job easier. You never know if the press will use all the content you have prepared, but if you have carefully prepared your thoughts and positions, a good reporter can craft a good article from it. I just try to make it easy for them, which in turn helps me become more visible.

If you are in a town with radio or television stations, take your press release to them in person, but don't be surprised if they ask you to sit down for a quick interview, so they can get some sound bites. Careful preparation ahead of time will make this work for you as well. They may even want you to go live on the air, as they need to fill airtime. Have your thoughts in order, and also written down so you can refer to them. No one will fault you for referring to notes. The President of the United States reads his statements and he has 27 people who prepare these briefings for him. You can do the same just on a smaller scale.

Depending on community size, you might get lucky and get some great exposure from the press and media. The secret is to prepare ahead of time and recognize the opportunity when it presents itself. At the early stages of the elective process, you need as much visibility as you can find, and working the press well can help you obtain it.

Also, keep in mind that whatever you do say is fair game to be printed or recorded, and may be used on the air, or in the newspaper. That being said, always carefully preplan what you are willing to say on various issues, write it down and don't be afraid to refer to your written comments. That way you won't get caught with your pants down and be misquoted in front of the public. You want to control the press rather than have them control you. Think about it before you put yourself in those situations. The good public relations exposure you can receive is well worth the effort as it will place your name in front of the public and you will be seen as a viable candidate.

Build a Campaign Timeline

Now that you have filed your papers and organized that Committee, what should you do next? Typically you will only have a few short months to promote your candidacy, identify issues, woo the voters, and get elected. To get things really moving you should build a reverse campaign timeline, starting with the election date and working backwards to the official filing date. All that open space in between those two dates, usually about three to five months, is where the strategy must be crafted and unfold with the help of your Campaign Committee.

This Campaign Timeline can be as easy as drawing a line on a long piece of paper, marking in the months, weeks and days, and then filling in the blanks. Or, you could just use a monthly calendar that has a lot of space in each day block so you can fill in activities, deadlines and major events that will need to take place. Your start date and the actual election become the two bookends holding together all the components of your quest for public office. It looks basically like this and can be embellished as much as need be:

- **Twenty-two Weeks (22) before Election Day**

1)
2)
3)   fill in the blanks
4)
5)

- **Twenty-one Weeks before**

1)
2)
3)   fill in the blanks
4)
5)

- **Twenty (20)—Weeks before**

1)
2)
3)   fill in the blanks
4)

- **Nineteen weeks (19)……then Eighteen (18) Weeks before…**
- **…. all the way down the sheet to**
- **One Week before Election**
- **Election Weekend**
- **Day Before Election**
- **Election Day**
- **And Victory!**   (Always keep your eye on the goal)

Then, you start filling in the blanks with all the planned components that you hope to undertake. Things like: filing days, press functions, speeches, door-to-door campaigning, coffees, special events, festivals, dinners, school events, etc. You want to pre-plan all of your expected activities and then add others as they develop. It becomes an important tool that constantly gets updated, only limited by the time you can commit, and your campaign treasury. You decide how active you are going to be, but this changes depending on what your opponents end up doing. You need to adjust to their activities and fight fire with fire. If they go door-to-door you may have to do so as well. If they give speeches at the school, you will want to do it too.

A good way to keep track of all these potential events and activities, is to set up a Scheduling Criteria Form, that you and your committee use to commit your time to various campaign events. National candidates have such criteria forms because the candidates are often in high demand and their committees have to try and get the largest exposure out of every moment of the candidate's time. On the local level it still works the same way. You don't want someone to commit you to a Coffee when you have accepted a speaking engagement. A poster sized Scheduling Calendar should be the official document that records information about various commitments such as speaking engagements, coffees, parties, school events, and public forums.

The Form should ask standard questions about who, what, where, and why the candidate should participate in an event. Then you find out who will be there, how much campaign literature should be taken, what else may come out of the event and then get it posted to the master timeline. In this manner, the candidate always knows where he or she needs to be and what is expected. You should also be selective, so you don't walk into a bad situation, but you want to post as many events to this timeline as you can comfortably handle.

This Campaign Timeline and Schedule should be flexible because it will change, as outside influences dictate changes. A donor that offers additional contributions late in a campaign may allow you to do an extra mailing, or buy another hundred signs. Or, because your opponent is planning to go door-to-door, you will to have to do the same. These kinds of changes will affect how your timeline actually plays out. It becomes a living document. Your timeline should be developed to ramp up your campaign slowly, building interest and gaining visibility day-to-day, as you get closer to the Election.

Candidates should always try to peak their campaign efforts just a few days before the election. That's when you will garner the most interest from the general public, who will then be more willing to pay attention to the election issues. In the many months prior to the actual election date you will find there is often general apathy on the part of voters. It is your job to get them interested in you and the issues.

I encourage you to actually develop a number of timeline scenarios, with contingencies for the various ways a campaign could turn or actually play out. You should have your committee develop a standard plan that takes a straight forward approach, presuming that everything will go as you have planned it. Then you should also develop a drop-back-and-punt emergency plan that factors what happens if an additional candidate files, if someone gains a major endorsement, or decides to send five major mailings to voters. Then develop an aggressive plan of attack, also as a fall back in case a major curve gets thrown at you and you have to pull out all the stops to be elected. The bottom line is your timeline needs to be flexible enough to deal with contingencies that will occur during the course of the campaign. And then proceed forward employing what you need to insure victory.

A number of basic activities have to be penciled into the timeline because you know the activities will definitely occur. Things like weekend door-to-door campaigning blocking out most Saturdays and Sundays, sign and brochure printing deadlines, press conferences, and candidate speaker nights. Then you should block out the Tuesday nights that the elected council meets because you need to be there to learn more about the issues and to observe the incumbent at work. Posting these events alone will chew up a big bunch of the time you have available between the start of the race and election day. Seeing and scheduling these activities will allow you to pace yourself, stay ahead of the competition, know what types of brochures and signs you will need to have, and know that your neighborhood coverage is expanding.

You should also pre-schedule your prep work and the mailings you intend to do to all known voters to arrive at their homes on specific days. This will assist in planning manpower support as well. If I have the luxury of a lot of help on that final Saturday before the Tuesday election, I might schedule a door-to-door literature drop rather than a mailing to save postage cost.

Two to three weeks before the election I will always plan on putting out my yard signs all at once and that can chew up a whole weekend of activity depending on the sign numbers and locations. You might ask why I would put signs out only two to three weeks before an election? I will answer that later on in my chapter on the art and science of yard signs.

Timeline Flexibility

In one recent campaign, after filing my papers, I found that six individuals had signed up to run for the three positions available. I immediately went back to my timeline and changed my emphasis in the coming weeks. My career work would take me out of town one whole weekend for a business convention, and my spouse had us going to an out-of-town wedding on another weekend. That was going to really cut into my ability to ring doorbells and introduce myself to voters.

I decided to adjust my campaign timeline by placing greater emphasis on meeting voters in new subdivisions where I could look for new voters. I also decided to put greater emphasis on identifying good sign locations early in the campaign because I might not be able to find them later and visit all the constituents. The important point was that I quickly adjusted what I needed to do for the campaign. You have to make your timeline flexible enough to deal with the curve balls of the campaign. It could be something as simple as a broken leg, a snowstorm or a flood that completely wipes out your ability to campaign. How you recover and adapt determines if you can win the election.

In my most recent campaign, an opponent who is also a good friend, had a heart attack a few weeks into his campaign and went under the knife to repair the damage. His recuperation would easily run through the actual election. While he was still in the hospital, his wife, kids and fellow Trustees including me, got together to plan out his campaign strategy while he was recuperating. He would be unable to get out there himself but we could on his behalf. So we coordinated for him and got him re-elected. He also has his health back and is as feisty as ever.

Going door-to-door will take up a major chunk of weekend time over four months. Over the years I have come up with an equation that calculates the time needed to do this important activity. You count the number of homes you have to cover and divide that by the number of weekend days you have available. That number is what you need to visit each weekend day. If you are serious about visiting everyone, it will be your biggest single time consumer, but I am a believer in the power of pressing the flesh and burning shoe leather.

With a full time job, you have to keep all this in perspective as well, because you need that job after the election is over. If you are a stay at home person you may have more planning time for behind the scenes work, but the actual campaigning is pretty much limited to some evenings and weekends. In any campaign you should also schedule some family time, as they will want to remember who you are and need to know your still around. Suffice it to say the Timeline is one of the most useful campaign tools you can use. Time is your enemy and by parceling it out carefully you can stay ahead of your opponents.

Know Your Opponents

One of the first assignments that you and your Campaign Committee should undertake besides raising funds is to figure out who your opponents really are. If Abe Lincoln thought it was important then you should too! It will help you figure out what needs to be accomplished to win the election. This is true whether it is one other candidate or a whole host of challengers.

In a recent national election, a candidate hired a full time video person to follow around his key opponent, recording his every move, his public comments and all of his activities. It unnerved the candidate and caused quite a ruckus in the press. While this is extreme, it can provide insights into how the other candidate will manage his or her campaign.

A candidate should make a concerted effort to learn as much as possible about the opponents and especially about an incumbent. For non-incumbent challengers I encourage you to ask your committee to do some research and background inquiries with friends and neighbors. Find out what type of work the candidate does, or why they are running for office. Their career work choice can help size up an opponent. If a candidate is an attorney you have to figure they understand the law and may have good insights into issues. If an opponent is a local realtor he or she may know all sorts of people in the neighborhoods. If an opponent is a teacher, you should find out if they teach in the district, because you have to figure the parents of all the kids will vote for their kids' teacher. If they do not work and are a stay at home parent, find out how active they are in the community and how deep their strength runs. A person who is head of the Parent Teacher Association, or a prominent member of a church will have strong community ties and will have a number of people they can call on through their school or church contacts. This information is important, as it will allow you to devise campaign strategy to oppose them.

One good way to explore your opponent's views is to snag a copy of their campaign literature early on to see what values they place where. Your committee members can call their friends and see if they can pick up a brochure or have someone else call and ask for one. If your opponents are going door-to-door and leaving campaign literature on doorsteps, do not just lift one as that would be unethical. Invariably, someone will also be watching you do so. That would hurt your campaign before you get started. Instead, ask the homeowner for it and explain why you would like a copy. That is being honest and if the homeowner gives it to you then you have acquired it legally.

If you are campaigning and run into opponent literature left in doorways, don't remove the materials, or destroy them. Such action would be counterproductive and may give your opponent something to talk about and destroy your reputation. In a situation like this, leave your piece next to your opponent's brochure, or if the homeowner should answer the door, present both items to the homeowner and encourage them to compare the two. When no one's home I place my campaign material right next to the opponent's and hope the homeowner will review both and make that comparison.

By learning the motivations and strategies of your opponents, you are in a better position to counteract their campaign efforts. If you know that a candidate intends to do all his campaigning by mail and phone, you will need to wage a door-to-door campaign, showing your face to every voter, hoping that the face-to-face contact will make a stronger impression than a phone call during dinner. When you are running against an incumbent, you will usually be able to find out all sorts of things about the person because there is a public record in the form of meeting minutes and voting records. There will also be newspaper articles that will tell you how the person perceives issues, and what positions he or she has taken in the past. If the incumbent has gone through previous campaigns, his prior voting record will give you some indications about how he will vote on issues when constituents are paying attention.

George Washington is the only President who didn't blame the previous administration for his troubles.

—Author Unknown

Oftentimes an incumbent will become more middle-of-the-road prior to an election, especially on fiscal matters, in order not to offend voters. If such changes in voting behavior can be identified, then you might want to point out how the voting record changed before an election. Voters might then notice the change as well. If your opponent changes his tune prior to an election, you may have found a soft spot to exploit, or you may find that you are sitting on the same side of an issue and you will not be able to challenge him.

Knowing these things up front can help you strategize how to gain the voters' attention and how to attack your opponent's record early on, rather than later in the campaign where you could be perceived as desperate. Remember, a lot of what you do or say, will be perceived by people with different points of view. Understand what those points of view are and you can be successful.

Knowledge of the incumbent's voting record is critical to developing an overall campaign strategy. You need to know where the incumbent is coming from in order to convert voters who elected that person in the past. You may position yourself as an alternative to more of the status quo.

Prepare a crib sheet or background paper on your opponent's track record, which can be obtained from public records, the official newspaper, his brochure positions, and the Library. You can also access the official minutes of the council by asking the clerk. Get a clear picture of the opponent's voting record. This information will be useful in debating issues, articulating positions, and in showing the public you know what you are talking about.

In your efforts to prepare this internal, for-your-eyes-only document, you want to look for major bread and butter issues affecting the community. That would include things like police, fire, water quality, safety, schools, garbage and streets. You want to have command of these issues because as you walk around people may ask about them, especially if they have become controversial.

As an example, ring a few doorbells on a street scheduled to be rebuilt or repaved and you will hear all sorts of positive and negative comments. You would want to articulate how your opponent voted on such issues, especially if you differ in viewpoint or you know that he was in the minority and took an unpopular stand. Try to set yourself apart from your opponent. Having his or her record handy allows you to differentiate your position with a voter. The only caveat to keep in mind is to make sure your facts are correct. If they aren't correct and you misspeak about, or slander your opponent, it will cause irreparable damage to your campaign and your personal credibility. Stick to black and white issues, actual voting records, and quotes that can be directly attributed to your opponent.

As you campaign, citizens may bring these issues up and then you can offer some insight on where you stand in relation to your opponent. With a dossier on your opponent, you will have such information at your fingertips. If you and your opponent agree on an issue, you may find that you are better off not drawing any parallel.

Try to find some way to attract the voters' interest so that he or she can differentiate you from the opponent, especially if the opposition is an incumbent known to the voters. This is most easily accomplished by asking some open-ended questions to determine other interests. An example would be, "So what are your opinions on this issue?" When you find an issue that allows you to take a singular stand, then see if you can encourage the voter to your viewpoint on the issue. If you do a good job of bringing him into your camp, the common issues both candidates agree upon may not be a factor.

When sizing up your opponents, you should also look into his or her school background, occupation, what kinds of community activities the person is interested in and what religious affiliation is involved. Religion should not enter into the race but you can bet that if your opponent is a church going person, his fellow parishioners will give him the benefit of the doubt. You may find that same concept will work in your church as well, and can be used to capture votes.

A person who has lived in the community forever and a day, and knows everyone is a formidable candidate and you will have to campaign harder to neutralize that factor. If you are the older or younger candidate it could be an issue that can be used to advantage once you have analyzed your district's demographics. If the older person is a dinosaur in a relatively young community, he or she may be out of step with community interests. If the community is an older staid community, a younger candidate may have to show that he is in step with the same community values to get elected. If your opponent is someone who is highly educated, more so than you, then he or she could look extremely competent in front of an audience, thus you may not want to encourage a number of public debates. Or you may be the one that is extremely comfortable in front of audiences, so you want to draw your opponent into those kinds of public forums and let people see you in action. Know who your opponent is and adjust your campaign style and approach accordingly.

All of these reviews will offer insights into your opponent and can affect the way you wage your challenge. I encourage you to leave no stone unturned because your opponent will be looking at your background in these same ways. He will be trying to exploit any weaknesses that you might have. By knowing his strengths and weaknesses ahead of time, you can build a flexible plan that will meet your objectives and get you elected.

Technology & the Internet

The next subject we should consider is how to best utilize technology, the computer and the Internet as major tools to develop good, effective campaign strategy. Over the last twenty-five years campaigning has gone from a pencil and paper manual art form to a truly remarkable electronic process that has changed the way communities elect candidates. And these technology advancements are continuing to change and improve election strategies as we speak.

Years ago, a candidate would have to do pretty much everything manually. He or she would sit for hours, carefully searching voter lists at the village hall, making notes, and paying for copies of lists to capture data. When developing a brochure, they would write campaign copy, have it typeset by a third party taking a great deal of time, have any photos screened by someone else and wait days and weeks to bring it all together in a presentable format. Then the printing process would first begin, which would take additional days before it would finally be ready for public exposure. Years ago if you wanted to communicate with citizens you sent them a letter or hoped that they were interested enough to come to a rally or speech.

Today, you can do many of these things yourself with a computer and a bit of knowledge. With a few keystrokes you can research data that is available on disks, manipulate the information, and sort it into useful blocks of information on your citizenry. You can create copy, make changes, use creative fonts and type, and have finished, presentable copy in a matter of minutes, if you know what you are doing. And, you can easily customize it even further for special events or because an issue becomes important later in the campaign. Today with e-mail you can converse with citizens almost instantly, you can gather opinions, seek their insights and tell them where you stand, all from your computer station.

If you don't have this kind of computer capability, you should find someone who can counsel you on all these technology issues, and show you your options. You need to get someone knowledgeable involved in your campaign. It could be your spouse or one of your children, or the computer geek next door. The secret is to find someone who knows how to navigate a computer and make it work to your advantage. Share with this person the various components, lists, maps and deadlines you have to work with. They will know how to assist you and you will be way ahead of the game.

Once this technical person has a feel for your goals and understands the parameters of what needs to be accomplished, they will be able to suggest all sorts of ways to gather information, sort lists, cut corners, and seek out the voters you need to be elected. This person will be able to show you how to save countless hours processing lists, developing campaign literature, issuing position papers, issuing press releases, and targeting potential voters.

Most of your campaign handouts can be created in simple Word document programs, and printed on your own printer at home or the office. If you don't have such equipment your local printer will. In most cities there are large copy shops and Kinko's stores that offer retail services for all sorts of computer oriented paper processes. They can scan and manipulate photo's, reduce, expand, size and ultimately copy documents. They can also do the printing, folding, collating and inserting that may be necessary. But all of these outside services can be pricey. So the alternative is to find the person who can help you do a lot of this stuff internally. Most of these documents can be easily handled on home computers with the right software and people coordinating, with a minimum of fuss.

Your various campaign lists can be sorted and downloaded in all sorts of useful formats. Years ago you would buy the voter election lists' from prior elections (not how they voted, just that they voted) and spend hours trying to manipulate them into effective campaign tools. Today you can usually buy these lists on a disk at the election commission or county and then have your computer person examine the files and sort them for you into the categories you need to use when walking the streets. The computer has changed the way campaigning is done and saves every candidate a great deal of time. Make the computer your friend and it will save you time and money in the long run.

More and more counties and local governmental units are making voter registration lists available for purchase. If they are for sale in your area, think about getting the data on a disk so that you, or your computer expert, can sort and revise the information to your specific needs. Invariably, this voter information will come in a format that isn't the most user-friendly, because the governmental units responsible for maintaining these records are using equipment that is often outdated and difficult to manipulate. If you can buy the information on disks, do so and let your computer whiz start working with it. There are all sorts of software programs like Microsoft Access and Excel that can be used to organize the voter data in any format that you want; in street order, by active voters, locations with signs, and block by block.

Website Campaigning

The political website is an even more recent adaptation of technology that has been embraced by politicians and candidates alike, to assist in building visibility and winning elections. From small town elected officials to presidential candidates, having an interactive website has become a crucial communications tool for reaching the public and waging an effective campaign.

During the 2004 Presidential primaries, Howard Dean used the Internet and a website to gain all sorts of support and connections with the public while his opponents did not embrace the technology, initially. He funded his primary campaign by using a website to great advantage developing a whole cadre of techie type followers who then used additional supporting sites to talk up the Dean candidacy, and the issues, while other candidates used more traditional campaigning concepts. The difference was the press embraced the concept of websites and personal blogs. It gave the press a way to interact with Dean and his site gave him great visibility with the younger computer savvy public. In the primaries he raised unprecedented amounts of money, on-line support and set up a vast network of avid supporters. In a few months most of the candidates for President had embraced this website technology for campaigning, opening up a whole new avenue of exposure and visibility. All of a sudden the political website had a front and center position in the public's mind and it changed the way candidates campaigned.

You can do the same thing with a website at the local level. It should be a priority matter for you to consider, well worth the start-up time, cost, and effort. The secret is to find the right person who understands all the technical website navigation issues, and get them on the team. You could even outsource or advertise for such a person if no one steps forward. I guarantee there are capable people out there who will want to help. If you can't find it internally, website development will be money well spent and becomes a legitimate campaign expense. It just means that you may need even more money than you thought.

This person will know how to get you started. All you will have to do is create all the background information and data you will need for the website screens and sub-screens. This will include your positions on issues, surveys, and personal information. I would create a sub-committee to handle this whole process and develop all of these materials based upon your local issues and the positions you intend to take. A good place to start is with the components that are going into your campaign brochure.

But you should also take some caution here, make sure you can live with what you put on the website, because once it is published, the comments and positions you embrace can take on a life of there own. You will have to stand by what you write and publish on the site because it will be readily in front of the public for all to see. So make your presented information clear and solid.

A website will give you a very visible platform on which to discuss issues and advise people where you stand. It becomes an interactive campaign brochure telling the public about your background, your roots in the community, your passion for certain issues, etc. Once you have embraced the concept of having a website then all sorts of possibilities open up and are available to you. You could encourage people to talk with you in a discussion format and send in their thoughts on the campaign issues. Every time someone does send a message, you can capture an e-mail address and can communicate further with the sender. Depending on their position, you could ask them to support your campaign, make a donation, put a yard sign up or simply remember to vote for you. But most importantly you can retain that e-mail address and remind them in the future to vote for you. As you make your site more inviting more people will interact with you and you will build a list of voter contacts. This is gold because it will cost you nothing to correspond with them while traditional mail involves considerable postage and time.

In recent years many communities and school districts have begun to utilize official websites to keep the public advised about what is going on in the community. These sites are used to post meeting notices, publish minutes, introduce elected officials and department heads, offer messages from the Mayor or Village President, and offer an interactive communications channel that has not existed in the past. Cities are also using community websites to let the public know who is on the staff, how departments are reached, and what is happening in the community.

Often this official site will have a section listing elected officials and their personal e-mails and websites. It could offer another line of communication. Savvy elected officials are recognizing that every time a citizen and voter sends them an e-mail, they can capture the e-mail address and have a great means of communicating with these voters in the future. This creates a great advantage for incumbents because voters are contacting them.

Keep in mind that not everyone has computer access, but that is changing as computer prices continue to become more affordable. Kids in school need computer knowledge and parents buy the units to assist them in their school activities. Depending on the affluence of your community, many families are already hooked up and on-line the Internet. And they are comfortable receiving information through this new method of communication. To speed up the gathering of voter e-mail addresses you could also set up various short survey questionnaires on your campaign website that encourages people to respond. You could talk about some controversial issue and ask for comments, or ask what the voters see as important issues. As people respond you build up a new contact list.

There is even a software program I have used called E-mail Extractor, which allows you to do searches thru major search engine databases to identify e-mail addresses that may be of interest to your campaign. With a tool like this you can find good e-mail addresses of voters and organizations without manually searching for them (eating up countless hours.) A word of caution though, while e-mail is an extremely inexpensive way of reaching voters you don't want to get voters angry, by spamming them with lots of un-requested campaign information, so be careful how you use these e-mail addresses. You don't want the voters to turn on you.

With this ever-growing e-mail list you can then advise them of campaign events, your timeline for election, and new positions you have taken as issues develop. You could ask them to support your candidacy, ask for assistance in setting up signs, or ask them to hold a Coffee on your behalf. The secret is to get a dialogue going with these voters. If they have the motivation to respond to your request for discussion of issues, or to comment on your website in general, they are interested people who will vote and should be pursued. A website can give you an edge that the other candidates may not have, and if you are not the incumbent, you need every edge you can identify.

On your website you want to present yourself and your credentials, show them a photo or two of you on the campaign trail, perhaps walking door-to-door, and then list the issues that you see as important in the election. The site can be as simple as that. The site will act as an electronic brochure that a voter can visit and wander through. Once you have the basic information about you and the campaign issues presented, then you can add other information like future campaign events, coffee locations you will be at, press conferences that will be held, and speaking engagements where you can see the candidates. This information allows the voter to get to know whom you are and hopefully become engaged in your campaign effort.

Since most websites can be presented in color on the computer screens, you should add some good color photos of yourself looking like a real candidate. This will allow the voter to connect with you. I will talk more about photo use when we start designing your brochure.

Your website should be kept as interactive and current as possible, with updates added to encourage people to return to the site on a regular basis. You should offer short surveys that people can respond to, offering you insights into what they are thinking and where they stand. Once the survey results are summarized, the results can be presented on the site encouraging people to return to find out what the public's consensus was. At the national level the presidential websites are updated hourly as the candidate travels, makes speeches, and interacts with the public. People become invested and care about the candidate if they can find out more about them. If you give voters a reason to visit the site they will do so and spread the word to others.

Finally, you should place your official website address, <u>www.(candidatesname) for(position).com</u> on all your written materials, business cards, campaign flyers and issue documents. In all your hard copy brochures and handouts you can encourage people to take a five-minute survey on-line that will help you understand how the voters feel about an issue. A survey gets voters to go to the website and gets them invested in your campaign. A website with survey information shows them you are concerned about their opinions. In this manner you will drive additional people to the site and then capture their e-mail addresses for additional follow-up. Building an e-mail list will be one of the most valuable things you can do in the campaign because it is the most inexpensive way to reach the public when time and money is a factor.

If you do develop such a website, think about crafting it so you could later convert it to your official elected website after the election. Such a site will be invaluable when you are trying to gauge voter sentiment on issues, and it will allow you to maintain future visibility with your constituents, since you will ultimately have to run again. That on-going e-mail correspondence list will become an even more valuable commodity as time goes by. You can use it as a call to arms, as a get out the vote list, or to respond to a crisis on a political issue.

I probably should have mentioned this earlier but there is a good magazine out there called **CAMPAIGNS & ELECTIONS**, out of Washington DC. Subscriptions are available for $50 per year. It has all sorts of useful information, trends and insights into the political spectrum. While it is focused on larger elections, including the Presidential and congressional races, much of the information presented has application at the local level once you process it down to your local level. I have found it to be a useful background publication to develop strategy and come up with ideas for my campaigns. The magazine can be reached at 202-207-0534, or 800-868-3638, or **www.campaignline.com.**

Demographics and List Management

"*Bad officials are elected by good citizens who do not vote.*"

—George Jean Nathan

In all political campaigns, clear demographic understanding and knowledge of your constituents is the name of the game. Good list management will help you determine whom the voters are, where your marketing efforts should be placed so that you don't waste precious time. Knowing your demographics will assist you in laying out a complete campaign strategy.

So what are demographics? The dictionary states that demographics are "the characteristics of human populations and population segments used to identify consumer markets". Simply put it identifies who the people are and where they can be found, and what basic identifying characteristics they will probably have. Once you have this kind of information, you will have better insight into how they can be approached and what may motivate their support.

In a political campaign and election scenario, demographics become the characteristics, habits and preferences of the population in your specific district, ward, or election area. That is, where are the voters, what are their politics, income levels, voting preferences, and will they actually turn out for the election. You want to know all sorts of things if the information is available. Are the voters liberal or conservative? Are they financially well off, or not so well off? Are they well educated or not? Are people even registered to vote? If they are registered, do they regularly vote in local elections? And if they do vote, do they vote in all elections? These are important questions and a good bit of this information is available if you know where to look for it.

A great place to look for demographic information and to get a feel for the power of these demographics is to visit the U.S. Census Bureau website and related sites that analyze all sorts of data, by area, by city, by zip code and a hundred other ways. The U.S. government officially gathers this information in a formal Census taken every ten years, which is mandated by Congress to keep track of economic and demographic information. In fast growing communities, there is often census data available from mini-census's authorized by the federal government that are taken by these communities every two or three years to reflect the expanding population growth. This information is worth looking at and analyzing to see how it can assist you in your campaign effort.

The Census Bureau offers valuable information on who we are, where we are located, where we have been, where we are moving, and how fast communities are growing. The official Census Bureau website is: www.census.gov. Take a look by coding in your zip codes. The information can be very useful. There are also other similar websites that can be useful in showing you what your community is all about. Try www.tiger.census.gov for all sorts of ways to analyze your district. Or just do a Google search and ask for Demographic census information on a specific area. The options will keep you busy for hours. If you want to get some insight into what your election district or community looks like all you have to do is put in a zip code in Google and start searching the data that appears.

After you have collected some data on your district, you should then look at old voting records. These are lists of who has voted in past elections in your district. You will find when you analyze past voting patterns, (I highly recommend that you do comprehensive research in this area), that everyone and their brother will turn out for a national election because of the tremendous amount of advertising and excitement that is created in a large, well funded national election. But the inverse of this is also true, if it is only a local election being held in an off year (not national, nor state), the turnout will be considerably lower, as many voters won't show up at all.

Ironically, citizens should be paying far more attention to the local elections. At the local level they have more input into the issues, and can affect the outcome with only 500–1,000 votes being cast. In a national election, an individual vote doesn't convey as much importance because the vote totals are in the millions. While the war on terrorism, inflation, and the latest TV shows is on everyone's minds, local issues should get far more attention because they impact people a heck of a lot more than these other topics will. Local elections deal with bread and butter issues that affect daily lives, things like streets, garbage, water quality, and community safety. This is where the demographics of a community play a role. You have to know your citizens and your neighborhoods to determine where the votes are and how likely people are to vote. With limited funding resources, you can't afford to visit every household with door-to-door campaigning, or to send everyone a mailing, because you would be wasting time and money, both of which are hard to come by.

So how do you find and identify these voters? In the old days, just 20 years ago, before computer record keeping became a part of every election, you would have gone into city hall, or the county, wherever past election statistics are kept and asked to see the results of prior elections. Since these documents were official records, they couldn't be removed from the premises but they could be looked at, reviewed and carefully analyzed.

You would take a morning off from work, buy a large cup of coffee and plan on spending hours carefully looking at prior voting lists showing names and addresses of registered voters, and determine whether they actually voted or not. You would not be able to see how they actually voted, but you could determine that these individuals physically showed up and pulled the election curtain lever to vote in past elections.

Identifying real voters is one of the most critically important research efforts you can undertake. In doing this exercise you will find that many people do not vote at all, and never will, for any number of reasons. It is one of the great tragedies of our democratic system. People enjoy so much freedom in a democracy that they do not value the most basic democratic right we have, the right to determine who will represent our interests.

> *"A citizen of America will cross the ocean to fight for democracy, but won't cross the street to vote in a national election."*
>
> **—William Vaughn**

If you don't believe me, just go out and ring a few doorbells and you will find out quickly that many people just don't care, have a huge chip on their shoulder, or are too lazy to exercise the most important right we have in our country, the very essence of democracy. Voter turnout is measured as a percentage of the qualified voters and you will be shocked to know that 50% of voters rarely show up.

You need to identify the 50% that do turn out for an election, as they are the people who can elect you.

The right to vote is by no means a universal right, but here in America our citizens often take this democratic right for granted. Having traveled on business throughout the world, including many third world countries, I can tell you this freedom to vote is a precious principle. People die each day trying to come to America just so they can enjoy these freedoms we often take for granted. And as a candidate you will meet all sorts of folks who are ambivalent about voting. It is a sad fact of campaign life. Thus, it is important for you to spend the time to identify who has truly exercised their voting rights. If you don't you will be wasting your time unless you are one very persuasive candidate!

When I look at past election voting records I look for similar election situations and patterns in voting numbers. If you are running in an off-year Spring election, you don't want to just use the prior November national and state election voting lists to determine who is likely to vote in the Spring election. Remember, I said the national election brings out about five times the voters, as a local election will turn out. If you don't recognize this difference in voting patterns, you will get give yourself a false sense of big turnout numbers going to the polls for your local spring election. But they will never show up. If you spend all your time chasing people who don't turn out, you will lose.

> *"Those who stay away from the election think that one vote will do no good: Tis but one step more to think one vote will do no harm."*
>
> **—Ralph Waldo Emerson**

While I will look at and use major election lists in my research, I will also go back farther in time and look for similar off-year elections to analyze. By off-year, I mean non-national, or state elections that involve local political offices and local referendums, like school issues, constitutional changes etc. The people who vote in these off-year elections are the people who will show up to vote no matter who is on the ballot. In campaign election circles these are the equivalent of the rock star groupies of voting. They are the real voters, the star-trekkies of elections, people you truly want to look for, identify, and talk to. And God bless these individuals because they truly comprehend what democracy is all about. These folks will turn out and vote for you if your pitch is solid and your passion makes sense to them. These are the hard-core voters who believe in the democratic process. You want to seek them out and go after them to win.

Hence the reason your demographic search is so important. It boils down to gaining efficiencies to make better use of your limited time and funding. Why waste valuable time and money seeking out voters who won't turn out for the election? Once you know where the real voters are located it is simply a matter of going after them. You can do that in all sorts of ways including direct mail, targeted calls and by visiting their homes. These folks are the ones that will get you elected.

Today, much of this information is computerized and can be sorted and downloaded into a variety of list formats, or can be captured and manipulated by your campaign committee to be even more useful. Again, you need to ask the keepers of this lection history what kind of specific information they have available and whether it can be purchased. The costs can vary but it will be money well spent so you can focus in on the true voters.

List Management

You will still need to buy a complete list of all potential voters by street address and name, whether they have voted in the past or not. Once you have analyzed this list against the real election voting history, you can start to refine all this information into a target list for follow-up action. There are numerous software programs that will allow you to manipulate all of this information to your specific needs.

After you have identified the likely voters in similar past elections, make copies of the voter lists and arrange them in street order. These lists become your door-to-door street bible or hit list, because it gives you the registered voters names and addresses up and down each street. If you can buy a list of who actually voted then do so. The current lists from my home County have voter history listed for the last four elections and have their phone numbers as well. It doesn't tell me how these citizens actually voted, only that they showed up and pulled the lever. If you can get phone numbers, they are a big bonus. These could be used to set up phone calling trees for volunteers to make reminder calls the weekend before the election. You should try to get any and all information you can on voters in your district. The more demographic information you have the more insight you can glean from your potential voters.

Once you have purchased these lists or the CD, make a whole bunch of copies so that they can be used in a variety of ways. Use one for your all purpose street bible, another to keep an accurate record of all my sign locations, and another to break apart in sections to assist door-to-door mail drops with campaign workers.

In your jurisdiction, if you can't buy copies of the lists, because it is an official document, then consider manually comparing the official list and make up your own copy version. It is a lot of work but the payoff comes when you are armed with information that your other opponents may not have. When purchasing these lists you will need to be specific as to which voting wards or precincts you want to obtain. Invariably you will also get voters that are outside your particular jurisdiction. They may be in the neighboring town but vote where you do, or they may be in the unincorporated township outside your village or city. While these names will be shown on the list you want to determine the computer coding that will allow you to discern the true eligible voters from the others.

Sorting the list for real voters is important because you have limited time and funding. You don't have time to chase voters who can't actually vote for you even if they wanted to. Again it's a matter of asking the right questions of the County or city computer programming people to understand just what the coding all means. Ask your questions clearly and they will help you understand what you can get.

In my hometown, the polling lists have a series of specific tax codes that determine where the various taxing authorities send the tax dollars once collected. As you might expect the codes are pretty accurate because they are dealing with who gets what tax dollars. Once you know the specific tax codes that correspond to your community, you can carefully eliminate the other names and addresses that are truly outside the district and concentrate on my specific voter block. That being said, you should still look outside the voting district for names of individuals on a key corner leading into town, or next to a school or high traffic area. Perhaps you could ask that homeowner to put up a sign for you and gain some visibility even though the homeowner can't vote for you. In my last election I visited three individual homeowners that were outside my district and asked them if I could put up my signs only on Election Day. Why? The homes were directly on the road leading to the voting location and it gave me one last impression before people went into the voting booths.

If you can't buy the lists its still worth the time to look at, copy, and work the official lists for your purposes. Get a strong cup of coffee, some colored marking pens and go to work highlighting the true voters. In many towns you are only talking in the hundreds, in larger communities you may be looking at thousands, so this may be a good time to have some friends who would help out. If friends do help, make sure you explain what you want them to identify or highlight so that the information is what you truly need, not just the opposite (that sounds like experience speaking doesn't it?).

When I am doing all this identification work, I use the different colored pens to identify corner house addresses, possible sign locations, and people who have said they will sponsor a coffee, or are willing to volunteer for some other activity. After a while my lists look like a rainbow, but if you know the coding the list is a treasure trove of important information when in the field. You want to see that the next house on the block is a hard-core voter, and the one on the next corner with a great sign location has already expressed some interest in your campaign. Such information will assist you in converting votes.

It is also a good idea to keep back up lists in a safe place. I have had my kids color on them, had coffee spill on them, and seen them blow down the street on windy days. These lists are valuable tools so once you have refined them, protect them and copy them so you have a back-up. You will find all sorts of ways to use them productively.

These doctored, marked up lists become your so-called hit list. The highlighted individuals are the folks that will actually vote and get you elected. All you have to do is visit and make them aware of your desire to be elected. See it's actually easy once you know what you are doing! So how do you use this list management to your advantage?

If you are doing door-to-door campaigning, attach a specific street of names/ addresses to your clipboard and start wearing out shoe leather. The beauty of the refined and marked up list is you can breeze right past the non-voter households if you are pressed for time. When approaching a house, cross-reference the address to your list. You will see that a Mr. Perry Clark is the voter in the household. When you ring the doorbell, its not just hello sir, its:

"Hi Mr. Clark, I'm Tom Renk and I'm running for Alderman. I hope you will consider me when you vote April 1st. This brochure will tell you more about me and what I believe in"

You won't believe how often the person will be momentarily confused and speechless about how you knew their name. In that moment of confusion you have a chance to get a few words in before the conversation ends with the door slamming in your face. (More about campaigning later, including what to do when a naked person answers the door, and how to accomplish your mission without creating an incident.)If your list is not accurate and the person you thought lived there has moved, you may get a new name and you can correct your list. It may also mean that the person has not registered to vote because they are new residents. This is a great opportunity to advise them how to get registered......so they can vote for you.

In most communities you can register to vote at the village or city hall, and often at the public library. In some communities it might also include the police or fire station. This is another question you should ask the city clerk when you take out your papers. If you can share this information with a new resident, you may earn his vote because you have already done him a community service. I would take it a step further by offering one of your nomination papers to sign. Then gently remind him his signature presumes that he is registered and hopefully he will make the effort to do so.

With a street list you can also identify key locations that may be needed for signs. I am always on the lookout for corner houses that would make good sign locations to get better visibility in two directions. With a street and name list in hand you can make a note where the corner houses are and call them later, or do special follow up to see if they would put up a sign for you.

After you leave the doorstep, try to capture some quick notes on your polling list next to the name, concerning interest level, issues brought up, or volunteering for some activity. Then when you get home immediately put all these notes and names on follow up lists of potential donors, sign locations, or workers who might be willing to help. You might even write a handwritten note on a postcard thanking them for their time and offering some follow up to their issue, or asking for their help. That follow-up action will generate votes. Believe me, it works.

Mapping Out Political Boundaries

While you are analyzing your timelines and demographics you also need to clearly determine the physical characteristics of your ward or district. The way to do that is to obtain the best map available that shows all of the physical boundaries, street names, and peculiarities of the district. You can probably get a good map from your friend the village clerk, or perhaps from the police or fire department. Just ask.

Districts, wards and precincts can make for a confusing mapped area with various boundaries jogging in and out, cutting through alleys, and across empty fields and parks with little rhyme or reason. You will need to know where your boundary markers or line demarcations are, and where they aren't. This will become very important for identifying your voters.

U.S. Speaker of the House Denny Hastert's Congressional District just down the road from me, runs east and west for over 40 miles in a very narrow band of small towns and farming communities. In some places is just a 2,000 feet wide. It is probably a nightmare to know where every household is located, yet it is critical to identify these voters, because they are the people who can vote for you.

If you are in a district that has been recently re-mapped to adjust for population changes, the boundary lines may also seem quite odd, cutting back and forth, crossing streets, cutting through alleys and crossing empty fields. You need to know your area limits because you can wear out a lot of shoe leather walking where folks can't vote for you even if they wanted to. Get a good map from a knowledgeable source and know your district before you start walking. Spend an afternoon before the campaign actually starts driving to the many corners of the district and clearly understand where the lines are. A good map will outline where the district actually starts and ends, its primary corridors, retail areas, and where problems might be. Often a district will be divided down the middle of a street and if you aren't clear about where that line is, you may miss a bunch of real voters who would have supported you if they had met you. Make notes on your maps and then if need be, ask the Clerk if you have designated the district limits correctly. It is well worth the time and effort.

After you have the best map you can find, visit a large format copier location like a Kinko's reproduction store. Make a number of copies as large as you can. A couple copies will become master wall maps to chart progress. Make a couple more large copies that could be cut into sections of the district into workable chunks of territory relating to distances that you and campaign workers can physically cover. Develop your own literature drop routes for volunteers, clearly marking where you want them to go. That way people truly understand which streets and homes they are supposed to be covering.

If a good color map is attainable that might have important landmarks on it like schools, public buildings, parks, commercial areas and neighborhoods, use this as a master map to really lay out a war campaign. A map like this will give you even greater insight into where people congregate and where potential issues may be located. Often parking problems abound in retail shopping areas. Speeding issues arise especially near schools and parks where children play. All these notations and symbols will also help you feel that you know the district dimensions. As an example, if there is an important school issue in play, people concerned about schools probably live relatively close, and their kids walk to the school. People that dislike commercial corridors are likely to live across from them.

Heaven forbid that you have strip clubs or adult book stores in your neighborhood in a commercial or retail area, but you would definitely want to know they are there before you start ringing doorbells at the neighborhood houses across the street. The same is true if there are other so-called attractive nuisances in an area, like taverns, nightclubs or high traffic businesses that could anger homeowners.

A good map will also identify some peculiar wedge of land or street that is tucked away that may have hidden voters that would love to vote for you if they knew you existed. I once found a senior citizens home built on a dead end street that wasn't apparent from the voting records. I went in there and signed up a good number of senior voters, arranged for rides on election day, and earned myself a number of votes for the extra effort. I can't tell you the number of times people on dead end streets, or in far corners of a district have told me they had never seen a candidate come to their door, and if I was that serious, they would vote for me. The map showed me where to look.

Good maps will greatly help you determine how to physically cover the district as well in the limited time you have to campaign. If you plan on going door-to-door, I would suggest you try to estimate how many houses you can visit on a typical weekend day, and then divide that number by the number of homes to be visited from your active voter polling lists. This will tell you how many days you will need to commit to the effort.

A good rule of thumb is that you will use 4–7 minutes per household, including walking to and from residences, time at the door, and any conversation you have. A few residents may want to talk longer, or might invite you in, but on average, it will still work out to 4–7 minutes per household average. Once you have a feel for what you could cover in a day then you can do some basic math to obtain some vote numbers.

Door-to-Door Campaigning Equation

75–100 homes per day X 18 weekend days (available in the campaign) = 1,800 homes

This amount of homes can vary because of terrain, hills etc.

1,800 homes X 2 voters per household = 4,000 voters met

2 voters per household is about average

Out of 4,000 voters you can count on at least 15%–20% of them, or about 750 voters, to vote for you because they have personally met you. That personal contact can really make the difference. People like to think they know you. And if you try to introduce yourself to them they will remember you when the election is held.

In most small town local elections, 600–700 votes will usually win the election. I have had total vote counts as low as 372 and as high as 5,000. In larger districts and cities the numbers may be higher but the volume of households will also be higher. That means more shoe leather but the equation is still valid. Break it down into chunks of geographic territory you think you can truly cover in a particular day. The estimates may change when you go from tight apartment clusters to rural homes, spread out with long driveways, but you will get a sense for these things when you are using good maps to break the areas down. Then keep track of your progress from week to week and it will help you meet the seemingly impossible challenge. I used mapping to effectively plan out and visit each voter's household in all of my campaign victories.

You should also use one of those large maps you reproduced to tape to the wall at home or at the campaign office, and start creating a visual battle plan. The whole team should use it as a focal point. When Saturday rolls around, you just pick out a pre-established neighborhood to visit and go to it. Afterwards, when you get home, use a yellow marking pen and line out the areas you have actually covered on that big map. Do the same on each Saturday and Sunday, and after a few weeks, a good portion of the map will have been colored in. It will motivate you and your followers to keep going because you will have a visual record of your progress.

I will talk more about this important subject, but suffice it to say that door-to-door campaigning is the Boston Marathon of getting elected, and all you wear out is your back and shoe leather. When going door-to-door it is important that you appear to be visiting all over the district. By having a good map you can pick out different areas and go back and forth across town. This can have a devastating psychological effect on all your opponents' as they will receive reports from friends that you were all over town and in the neighborhoods. If they aren't out there as well, you will put great fear in their minds and defeat them before they get started.

You should also be sure to visit all your opponents' neighborhoods early in the campaign if for no other reason than to show them you are out there. Don't shy away from walking right up to the opponent's door and their immediate neighbors' doors. You may not get their votes but you make them fully aware of your candidacy. They will report to the other candidate that you were there and are very serious about the campaign. It sends an important message to all of your opponents.

Then again, some of your opponent's neighbors may not actually like the other candidate for any number of reasons, and would gladly support you. When you run into that situation, exploit it in as many ways as you can. Ask them to put up a front yard sign, just because your opponent will have to stare at it day in and day out. Then ask them if they would sponsor a coffee so you can meet the other neighbors. Think of the psychological impact these activities will have on the neighborhood. You might even ask if the neighbor would distribute literature to their other neighbors.

An excursion into the enemy camp may also be a great opportunity to find out more about your opponent and potential weaknesses. It's kind of like a reconnaissance mission going behind enemy lines to do covert work. And doing so can demoralize the heck out of your opponent. I highly recommend it, but also encourage you to do such work in a dignified positive way.

Campaign Finance

In order to run an effective campaign, you need funding support. You will need about $20 million if you are running for Congress. But if you are running for local office, the costs come way down to real world figures, oftentimes less than a thousand dollars may do it, although you can still spend up a storm if you want to, or you have opponents that want to throw money at the electorate. This too is one of those areas where custom may dictate how much money will have to be spent to get the job done. I'm always intrigued with national level politicians who will spend millions of their own money to get elected to $185,000 jobs. They must have their reasons but that is another story.

Let's get real and talk about the money you will need for an aldermanic race, a school board election, the local judicial race, the County Board seat, or the race for Mayor in a small town. This is where the real political action is.

You will need money for campaign literature, which may include design and printing. You will need postage money to mail these brochures, and perhaps envelopes to put the documents in (although there are ways to eliminate both costs). You will need money for campaign signs, the printing and the stakes as well as hammers, nails and staple guns to set them all up. You may need money for advertising, as well as all sorts of promotional giveaways. And you will need money for fund-raising events to make more money.

Much of this potential expense will be dependent on how much the other candidates expect to spend. If you have a half dozen candidates all running for the same office, a horse race occurs before the Primary Election and it is usually a name recognition race. In this situation you will have to spend dollars fast just to gain name recognition and visibility. If your opponent is a well entrenched incumbent you may have to spend even more to gain that name recognition. The bottom line is you need to recognize that money is a necessary part of the election equation, even at the local level.

Throughout the United States there are Campaign Funding laws that dictate how election donations and money can be gathered, contributed, recorded and spent. Usually the laws are quite extensive and may at first be very intimidating. But they actually aren't that difficult to understand for all of us law-abiding citizens who understand that only the federal government deficit spends. In local elections you only spend what you have available. Campaign laws have become a part of state and federal law because over the years some candidates, at various levels of government, have been less than honest where their funding sources have come from. They have not reported large donations from people they may be beholding to, or have misspent campaign treasuries, and have lost the public's trust.

You <u>must</u> take the time to become aware of Campaign Finance laws, and in most cases you can get that state law information from your Clerk. If you still don't understand what is required in order to meet state requirements, this is when you may want to get your campaign committee together, and hope that you included an attorney or accountant that can make sense of all the laws that you must adhere to. Such a person would also make a great Campaign Finance Chair to assist you with processing donations, recording expenses and meeting filing deadlines. In some states there are financial limitations that dictate when financial reporting kicks in and you are required to make periodic reports. In Illinois, if your total dollar volume spent will be under $500, you are not required to go through all the formal filing requirements. I still recommend keeping meticulous records of all donations, transactions and expenses. In Illinois if you go over that amount then you must follow all the financial filing requirements. You should always ask if and what dollar limitations exist in your state. In an uncontested race, your expenses are minimal, whereas in a heavily contested race, you may spend a lot of money just keeping up with your opponents.

With good luck you may receive small and large donations from family, friends and neighbors. You may find that there are also special interests out there that believe in what you believe in and would like to see you elected. Support from these special interests can be perfectly legal, but this is where the campaign finance laws come into play. The rules will dictate how much can be given, how it is to be presented and the procedures for recording the donation. The laws are written to create a paper trail that can be reviewed by the public, with the premise that if everything is out in the open and available for scrutiny, then the potential for hanky-panky is minimized. So you need to pay attention to the finance rules so that you can accept such contributions.

At the same time, there may be situations where you do not want to accept a donation because you feel it will compromise your position, or you do not want it to appear that you are supporting some position, issue, or question. That is perfectly acceptable behavior on your part and you are within your rights to politely say no thank you if you feel it will create future problems or suggest some bias on your part.

These campaign finance regulations and procedures are meant to protect you as a candidate. Use them well and you will have no legal problems or challenges to the way you are running your campaign. I always recommend that you get your Finance Chairman involved in these issues so that you can concentrate on campaigning. Just don't ignore staying on top of all the campaign finance reporting responsibilities.

Budgeting

All campaigns cost money and you will be shocked at how much everything will cost when it is all said and done. You can spend hundreds of dollars without even trying hard for political signs, brochures and postage. And that is just the basics. The best way to get a handle on the amount of money you need to fund your campaign is to build a budget. I recommend that you start with a bare bones basic budget, the minimal dollars you think you will need to win the campaign. You don't want to make a good showing, you are in it for the win.

First, give some thought to what will be necessary to compete with your opponent(s). Just having a number of opponents will increase the cost factors, as you have to buy more signs and brochures. Then you have to consider how much manpower may be needed, can be handled by volunteers, or will you need to buy some service help. You have to estimate the cost to write and create the brochures for distribution and mailings, and then add in the costs of typesetting, photographs, copying and folding these brochures. To introduce yourself to the public you will have to factor in some public relations, and perhaps advertising, or consider the costs of developing a website. Then there are the expenses for materials, gasoline and shoe leather. Don't forget you may have to offer food and drink to campaign workers, because it is a real cost that is often forgotten about and then it comes out of your pocket. Heck, you should also figure in the cost of a victory party to set the right tone for the whole campaign.

A basic budget adds up fast and looks something like this:

Campaign Literature

Primary pocket brochure, design & printing-2,000 copies	$700
Postcards and door-hangers	$200
Yard signs, stakes and materials-500 signs	$ 1,000
Postage, first class and bulk permit	$300

Custom printed envelopes	$100
Various District Maps and copying	$ 75
Polling Lists and reproduction	$200
Campaign Events, dinners, coffees	$250
Advertising in newspapers, local CableTV	$1,000
Phone calling—cell phone use	$200
Election Day expenses, Van Rental	$ 75
Election Night Victory Party (beer wine and chips)	$250
Total	$ 4,350

A campaign budget adds up quickly. A sample budget like this covering just the basics can get you into substantial money in no time at all. If you do not believe you can raise that kind of capital in your community you have to start cutting back on the various expense categories.

The first thing that could be cut out of this budget is the advertising because it is expensive and I have never found it to be that effective. Advertising works well when the entire community receives the paper. In my area, the newspapers are outside the immediate community and you pay for exposure with voters who cannot vote for you. The money is better spent on focused marketing efforts like door-to-door campaigning, brochures and signs.

After eliminating advertising, look at ways to trim other costs. The real key to election success is to target the real voters. By zeroing in on these hard-core voters, you maximize the impact your limited dollars have rather than chasing non-existent voters. Rather than a car or Van to take people to the polls on election day, line up some campaign supporters who could drive people themselves and set up a car service. See who on your Campaign Committee might have computer design experience and see if they could design the campaign brochures.

But don't skimp on yard signs and the primary campaign brochures because they are very necessary tools of the trade. They give you the most bang for your buck, and visibility and name recognition is the name of the game. Put your money where you will derive results that can be measured by the number of signs up, the number of voters and houses covered and the number of votes ultimately received.

When you do draw up your first budget, start with everything that you would like to do and try to get good estimates of what it will all cost. Once you know how much you could spend then you have a good target of what you would like to receive in campaign donations. As funds come in you can add additional budget considerations to the mix. If they don't come in you can take things out of your budget as needed.

Your budget has to be flexible as well because you haven't even thought of all the other things you will need to mount the campaign. You will invariably need every cent for campaign emergencies that you can't possibly foresee now. You will need to pick up all sorts of supplies like a good set of long underwear, an extra staple gun, maps and mapping supplies, clipboards and rubber bands, letterhead, envelopes, stamps, wood for sign stakes and large signs. It never stops.

Fundraising Events

Once you have an itemized proposed budget you can then determine how you will try to raise these funds. To kick off one of my campaigns, I held a poker party for my neighbors in the basement. Couples were invited and all the spouses decided a smoke filled basement was the last place they wanted to be so we had neighbors on two floors. I promoted it as a political fundraiser so people knew what they were getting into before arriving, and I asked them to contribute a $25 donation to the campaign. All the beer, snacks, and sandwiches were on me. I was already spending money to make some.

The party worked out beautifully because many of my neighbors insisted on giving me larger donations, and I was on my way. Besides everyone having a great time I lined up a bunch of campaign helpers to assist with signs and handing out literature. It was great way to let the neighborhood know that I was a candidate. They liked having a neighbor who was running for office. By the way everyone also signed my nomination papers.

There are many ways to design campaign fundraising events. You could try sock hops, bowling parties, bake sales, spaghetti dinners and the proverbial pancake breakfast. They have all been used effectively. These can be especially valuable if the event components are also donated. That way you aren't spending a lot to make a little. When contemplating some special fundraising event always ask if the vendor would donate something towards the event. In a bowling alley it may be a free line of bowling with every admission. In a bar it may be a couple kegs of beer from the owner. At a neighbors house it might be that they would donate the food and snacks. If the local baker is a good friend maybe you could ask him to donate all the donuts for a breakfast fundraiser. But also remember that all these in-kind donations must be recorded as donations to your campaign and have a real financial value.

The secret of such events is to let your imagination run wild, don't be afraid to ask for help and favors, and promote it to all your friends and neighbors. Encourage them to bring their friends and you have the makings of a great campaign party. Keep it as non-political as you can and the neighbors and friends will appreciate the low-key approach. They will usually ask you how they can help and then you can invite them to participate in all sorts of ways.

At such events you should have campaign literature available and sign-up sheets for the various activities you are contemplating so that people can get involved and kick off your campaign with a bang. But never push this stuff on people. Instead it is available and sitting on a table for them to pick up if they want to. In the corner near the door, campaign signs could be stacked up and ready to go. People grab them on the way out, although you want to find out who is taking them so you know where they are.

Campaign Coffees

In any campaign, be it at the local or national levels, the secret of success is to meet as many people as possible, press the flesh, and let them get to know you. You can do this in all sorts of ways and special events can often double as fund-raising efforts as well. When you hear the term 'coffee' in a campaign it doesn't mean that the whole committee is going to hold it's meeting at the local Star-buck's. A Candidate's Coffee is a small neighborhood group meeting of voters invited to someone's home, usually in the district, to meet the candidate and hear more about the issues and campaign. The sponsor is usually someone who has volunteered to bring his or her neighbors together in an informal meeting to get to know you. They have been called coffees because in most cases coffee is served along with other light refreshments. Usually the sponsor takes on the cost respon-sibilities for the refreshments. If this is uncertain, ask so you don't embarrass yourself or your host.

In most cases only 12–20 people will be invited to keep the atmosphere infor-mal and relatively one-on-one. These folks are usually immediate neighbors of the host and are invited by them personally. The candidate will usually make only a short formal presentation at about the mid-point of the scheduled time frame, and most often will mingle with the guests to listen to their views. That way the guests can come and go as they need to and the candidate can work the room.

Scheduling a number of these events during the course of a campaign is a good way to get your message out to the public and keep the momentum moving for-ward. Since most of your neighborhood campaign activity will occur on the weekends, when people are home, coffees' give you a good way to productively meet people during the middle of the week. Mid-week campaigning is tough because people are less likely to want to answer the door when they are putting the kids to bed or relaxing after work. A coffee brings these folks out to a special event on a night when you wouldn't be able to get out there and campaign. It is also a great way to meet people in other parts of town, securing new sign locations, helpers and donations.

Coffees are also a great way to increase your campaign donations. The secret is to keep the donations small so no one feels threatened or out of place. People meeting you for the first time may be reluctant to give you a large donation, but will comfortably write a check for $10 or $20 dollars after hearing your message. Your host could start the donation ball rolling by quietly writing a small check and handing it to you without a lot of fanfare. People will notice and realize they can do the same thing. Thank them as well and that will generate a few more. I have received up to $100 a night from various local coffees over the years, and I consider the time very well spent. The other thing to keep in mind is that if someone actually comes to a coffee, they are probably in that true voter category. You have an excellent chance to gain their support because they will get to see you in a positive light and will remember you when voting.

Some elected officials think coffees are overrated because they take up a lot of time. While that is true, I have found coffees' to be a great way to explore new neighborhoods or other parts of town. Just find a couple of friends or acquaintances willing to sponsor such an evening event. They will usually send out informal invitations or flyers to their neighbors. Give everyone a week or two notice so your attendance will be good. Try to schedule a couple of coffees' in every neighborhood to get a good word of mouth campaign started. It is also a great way to terrify your opponents because they will hear that you are all over town and building strength right in their own backyards. Coffees' allow you to meet new groups of people and expand your organizational depth.

At a coffee always have campaign literature available to distribute along with sign up sheets for various campaign jobs that will be needed down the road. Ask the host to put up a yard sign that evening so the guests will see what they look like and may be comfortable having one in their front yards later in the campaign. If signs are going up on a particular weekend get their names and addresses and tell them you will put a sign up when all the others are planted three weeks before the election.

Often you will find that another guest will offer to hold another coffee in their immediate neighborhood. Then you pull out your timeline and schedule and find a night that you can do it. One coffee will generate another one and you gain greater exposure. Coffees are a great way to introduce yourself to a larger audience and get your campaign message out in an otherwise dead time-period in mid-week.

Funding Your Campaign

There are only two basic ways to fund your campaign. The first way is obvious, you simply reach into your own pockets and fund it internally. The second way is to have other people pay for your campaign. I prefer the second way as my funding resources have always been limited with mortgages, children wanting to go to college, and such.

Occasionally you will hear about a wealthy person who actually does fund their own campaign to gain a seat in the Senate or the House, but most of us don't have that kind of pocket change lying around. The simplest way to fund your campaign is to pull out your checkbook and pay for it yourself. But I don't recommend this approach. First, you don't want to do so because of campaign finance rules and regulations. You also don't want to co-mingle your personal funds with any campaign donations that do come in. Only use personal funds if you can't come up with other donations from constituents. Over the years I have spent lots of personal money, but in doing so I have learned how to seek financial support from the people that hope to help elect you.

There is one exception to the use of personal funds and that is if your campaign finance laws allow you to formally loan money to your campaign to be paid back to you personally later out of donations. If your state allows this and the County Campaign Chairman should know, it would be an excellent way to get your campaign finances off the ground early in your campaign effort before much of your fund-raising has occurred. While you would use your money up front you could get reimbursed from other donations later on.

Use of personal funds may make it harder to create a clean, neutral paper trail and it might raise questions later on. While this may be the easiest way to meet your campaign funding issues, you will still have filing requirements that have to be met at specific times. And you can't just write yourself a check either. In most cases you want to isolate the funding dollars you personally donate and all the contributions that are made so that a paper trail is established. What you can do is write a personal check to your campaign fund and deposit it in a special checking account that is created for the campaign. While I will always write the first check to my campaign, I try to keep it small, as I may have to write others later on. I prime the cash pump and then seek other campaign donations to pay for the bulk of my expenses. The easiest way to manage the finances of the campaign is to create a separate bank account in the name of the Candidate. The **"Tom Renk Campaign Fund"** is the one that I have used for years as it allows me the flexibility to run for any office I choose.

If you name it the Tom Renk Village Trustee Campaign Fund, then you will only confuse people should you later on run for a different office. So I keep it simple and flexible. Over the years in a number of different locations, I have had banks that were nice enough to let the account go into dormancy for a couple years at a time, and then be reactivated when I needed to run again. But today, with all the new profit centers in banks they may not be as interested in carrying a dormant account unless you leave some minimum balance in it. In my most recent campaign my bank account requires some minimal activity at least once a year so it doesn't actually go dormant. Finally, if you don't want to keep track of such things in between campaigns you can always kill the account and just start over if you decide to run for office again. The only problem with this approach is that most accounts will want to print some minimal number of checks, usually in the hundreds and you will end up using seventeen checks during the campaign, and the rest all goes to waste. After the election make sure you destroy unused checks rather than letting them sit around and eventually get lost.

Talk to your local banker and ask if he would be willing to set up an account like that. You may be surprised that he sees you as a future politician he may need to work with and the bank will be more than helpful. But the only way to find out is to get an appointment and ask. Take the Campaign Finance Law information with you so the account can be set up to meet all guidelines and filing requirements.

If you do set up a bank account like this, it's best if you don't use yourself as the official signatory for the same obvious reasons. That's a job for your Finance Chair even if it is to be your spouse or brother. You want to be at arms length and have some checks and balances between you and the funds that will be coming in, and going out to pay for campaign expenses. Its cleaner that way and you won't have to worry that you will be challenged by an opponent or the State about how you are spending your own funds.

Now you have a campaign account that isolates all the campaign donations that will come in, including any money from yourself, rather than co-mingling such funds with your own personal finances. The last thing you want to do is to send your mortgage payment out late because you overspent on the campaign.

Building a Campaign War Chest

Now that you have set up your Campaign Bank Account, how do you go about getting people to contribute to your campaign effort? There are all sorts of ways to solicit support and build a campaign treasury to work with.

The easiest way is to simply ask people. The worst that can happen is they say no. Remember that Campaign Committee you created? Start with them at the very first organizational meeting. Quietly ask one of your most trusted associates, or friends, to make a rather public offering of a donation at the first meeting. Encourage this person to make the donation while everyone is discussing campaign strategy. Ask him to make it a reasonable amount that could be easily matched by others, say $50 or $100 dollars, and have him write out the check right then and there. You say thanks a lot and mention how much the dollars will help the campaign get off the ground.

Then watch as many of the others at the table pull out their checkbooks and match that same amount. It is called keeping up with the Jones'. The secret is to make sure the initial donor makes a reasonable contribution that can be easily matched by others without breaking their bank accounts. If the first donor wants to give you a larger amount, have him write a separate check in private so as not to scare off the others with some big dollar amount. Have him write that $ 50 check right at the table you are all gathered around. Before you know it you will have a couple hundred bucks to work with from people who are truly interested in helping. They only needed to know how to contribute and what would be appreciated. You are off to the races and at the very least will be able to pay for all those yard signs. Remember to thank everyone profusely so they can feel good about their contribution. Everyone will get excited and involved if you allow them to feel good about their donation.

The same approach works any time you are at a 'Coffee', or any of your meetings or fundraisers. Have someone you know well and trust, perhaps the person who volunteered to host the event for you, make a public donation, again for a small amount like $20 or $25, and others will readily get the idea and jump on the bandwagon.

While soliciting contributions, you should not be the one doing the initial asking or accepting, as you should stay neutral and above all this financial strategizing. If someone offers the check to you, thank them first, but then direct them to your finance chair for the actual transaction. Remember you want all these people to vote for you, so you want someone else to be the collector. But it is also very important that you publicly thank the special fund starter for his campaign donation, as that too will help people realize that their small donation is meaningful and greatly appreciated.

Another approach is to have your campaign chairperson act more aggressively and kind of strong arm everyone into donating some dollar amount, but coercion can breed contempt for you and your election, It may come back to haunt you later. I think it works better to have everyone want to volunteer some small amount once they know that it would be acceptable and well received. Keep in mind they have no idea what a campaign costs and will be uncomfortable shelling out $500 but would willingly give you $25 or $50. Make them feel good about doing so and your budget will be set. Everyone is willing to help once they know their small contribution will help!

Another approach I have used successfully is to develop a simple Campaign Flyer that basically announces my candidacy and encourages people to volunteer their support. It can be used as you seek nomination signatures, go door-to-door, attend a coffee, or make a campaign appearance. Always have them available so that if someone expresses interest in helping you can offer them a variety of help options. I ask them to consider supporting the campaign with a number of relatively simple options including:

1. Handing out literature in their neighborhood

2. Scheduling a coffee to meet their neighbors

3. Making a small donation of $25, $50 dollars to the Campaign Fund.

As you might guess, people won't be terribly excited about going door-to-door handing out literature, nor will they want to have people over to their house for a coffee, so they decide that making a campaign contribution would be the easiest and cleanest way to support the candidacy.

Remember to always keep the dollar contribution options low enough so that people are comfortable in choosing their dollar amount. This approach is always worth a couple hundred dollars only limited by the amount of flyers you send out. Figure you will get a 5–10% response on the number of flyers you send out. Lower the dollar options to say $10, $25, and $50 and the percent of volume should go up, as you will have made it easier for people to make a donation and support your campaign.

Scheduling a fundraiser or two is also a great way to collect campaign contributions. This could be on a very casual basis, like in a house party situation, or more structured, but it is important that you let people know what they are getting into before they arrive. You don't want them to think it's the regular weekly neighborhood party, or poker night, and then put them on the spot asking for money.

Think about having someone sponsor the event for you at his or her house, or at a restaurant or bar. Send out simple flyers or real invitations, inviting people to come to the event. Be clear in calling it a "FUNDRAISER FOR (candidate's) CAMPAIGN FUND" and people will recognize that they should bring their checkbooks, or some cash with them. Or simply have the flyer state that there will be refreshments (beer and wine) and that you are charging $20 at the door as a donation to the campaign. Using these methods you will get a lot of small contributions, but they add up quickly. When you do these kinds of promotion be sure to keep copies of the brochures, the invitations, or the flyers to substantiate how the dollars were received.

I mentioned the poker party earlier, but if it is a regular gathering among friends, and you pre-announce it is a fundraiser, you could also then ask the host to announce that to support your candidacy every other hand winning hand will share 10% of the pot with the candidate. Then keep track of the amounts earned and from which card winners and once the dollars get up to that comfortable $100 or $200 dollar level, you cut it off so no one feels as if they are being treated unfairly.

A word of advice, even if you have the best Royal Flush poker hand you have ever had, don't bet the pot up, as the card players will say you are just feathering your own nest. Also, the press would have field day with this card party fundraising approach, so make sure you are behind closed doors, and among good friends before and after the game. Better yet, take off the candidate hat altogether, play to win, and maybe you will be able to fund your own Campaign Fund.

If you have a good friend that owns a restaurant or bar, ask them if you could use the back room some night without cost for a fundraiser. Tell him you will buy a keg of beer and ask if he will donate one. You will be helping yourself and your friend's business. As a footnote on a situation like this, his donation of space (or even a keg of beer) may be considered an in-kind donation depending on what the campaign finance laws are. Such an in-kind donation is perfectly legal; it just needs to be recorded as a donation and placed in the right categories on the campaign finance reports.

Over the years I have had wonderful committee support and neighbor volunteers that took things even further. One couple got so involved they staged a neighborhood carnival party for me with food, drinks, and little booths for fundraising. They clearly called it a fundraiser and invited all my immediate neighbors, my friends from work and school and people that I didn't even know, offering a great excuse for a party. They offered games of chance for the parents and the kids, and cheap prizes.

They even had a whipped cream pie-throwing contest, and a kissing booth. I tried to be the guy in the kissing booth but my hosts had other ideas. As you might guess, who can pass up a political pie-throwing contest? I was the lucky guy who ran into all those whipped cream pies. The whipped cream itself doesn't hurt, it's the metal pie tins that really do the damage as the whipped cream is ground into your face. To this day I still don't like whipped cream!

It turned out my wife got to be in the kissing booth, and that was where all the real action was. All the neighborhood guys kept lining up at a dollar a kiss. With a lot of repeat customers she made more money than I did! But it was all for a good cause. An additional benefit was that I met a large group of new neighbors and they saw that I was a good sport and approachable. A couple people asked if they could make a campaign donation and again I suggested small amounts so that no one felt put out. One check led to another, and the next day I had to make a special trip to the Bank to deposit all the checks. Many of these wonderful people also joined the campaign team. Many of their kids even volunteered to help out with the literature drops that we scheduled later in the campaign. It was great event and well worth the whip cream bath!

My first tentative effort to run for public office back in 1976 was completely funded out of my own very shallow pockets. I remember I spent about $280 dollars, mostly on signs and brochures and lost in the primary a few weeks after I got started. After that, I tried harder to rely on contributions from friends and neighbors to fund all my campaigns without using personal funds. Over the years I have spent as little as $400 and as much as $3,000 for local elections.

I can't tell you any specific amount is too little or too much. Its one of those things you have to determine yourself, and it is dependent on your campaign needs. The advocacy of your opponents will somewhat determine the amount of effort and visibility you need to put into the election. Often you have to match your opponent blow for blow, item-by-item, activity-by-activity. If they decide to have 200 yard-signs, then they will potentially have greater visibility until you neutralize the effect by printing and distributing 225 signs. Thus, you will need extra campaign dollars to fund the effort, perhaps late in the campaign. I always keep that in mind when I am looking at fundraising.

If an opponent starts using car top carriers, then you may have to follow suit, or at least trump the move with an even better more visible approach. If they all of a sudden do a major mailing that costs a couple hundred dollars in postage you may have to match the effort to stay even. That's when having the ability to dig a little deeper with extra funding becomes so important.

You may have noticed in the large state and national campaigns that candidates spend many early months building up their war chests based on the fact that there will be unknown needs coming out of the election. Even at the local level that may be a good strategy to keep in mind.

In large political campaigns with Election Day just a couple weeks off, you will begin to notice that every other television ad seems to be for candidates running for major offices. This is when that large campaign war chest comes in handy to expose the candidates to the public. A political campaign starts building to a fever pitch about three weeks before the election and keeps expanding its efforts right up through the final weekend before the election. It's a game of one-ups-man-ship with both candidates jockeying for position and visibility.

While it doesn't get quite as crazy in a local election, the lessons learned by observing the larger political races can be helpful in plotting local strategy. The secret is to know what your opponent(s) are doing or are planning to do. Remember when you filed your papers and the candidates were casually talking about what they would be doing in the campaign. That information is valuable so you can mount an effective countermeasure to whatever they are planning. You may have to have additional campaign workers to deal with what your opponents said and that may mean more budget dollars and campaign donations.

Your Campaign Committee can help you in monitoring these situations. They should advise you when they see activities benefiting the opponents. Then you may be in a position to respond to the initiative. Responding to some activity may take some more money or a change in plans.

Always try to have more campaign funding available than you will need. You can always keep surplus funds that you do not need in the campaign treasury account for the next election. Or you can use such funds up with a great campaign victory party to thank all your supporters. Try to develop a worst-case scenario budget to identify the total financial outlay you may need to spend so you have a good campaign dollar target to seek from donors. This can be figured by knowing what my initial sign costs are and what it will cost to have the printer make up an extra hundred at a later date. Also figure what the costs of doing a second major brochure printing and mailing would cost, and what the costs of buying advertisements in the local paper will be.

By having all that information at your fingertips, and back up funding dollars ready to go, you can then counter any move your opponent should make, even if its on the eve of the election. I have even been known to have a backup brochure ready to be printed and a standing order for an extra 100 signs sitting with the printer ready to be activated on a phone call if needed.

But to make all this happen quickly you need to have the funding available, ahead of time. So make a strong effort to line up financial resources early on. Tap into your family for a few bucks, neighbors and friends that are willing. You also don't want to owe favors to any person or company after you get elected so keep donation amounts beneath the "I own you" amount that someone would give and expect a particular result from.

Big Donors Buying Votes

"If you once forfeit the confidence of your fellow citizens, you can never regain their respect and esteem. It is true that you may fool all of the people some of the time; you can even fool some of the people all of the time; but you can't fool all of the people all of the time."

—President Abraham Lincoln

At the local level you will have issues that may encourage contributions from individuals or corporations hoping to buy your vote. You must be very careful about whom you will accept money from. While garbage may not sound like a big deal, the garbage collection contract may be worth millions of dollars each year and the companies bidding hope to have a friendly reception. They may hope to influence candidates to make sure their lucrative contract gets renewed. They want to see their friends in high places, so to speak. Donors like this may even try to influence you by offering smaller donations through employees, some of whom may be your neighbors.

Thus, you have to be careful when accepting campaign donations. It is important to explore where the money is coming from, if such offers have strings attached, or if you are expected to vote certain ways on future issues. Always know what the pedigree of the donation is, and don't be afraid to ask where the money is coming from. You may have to turn down money because you know where it's coming from. The same is true concerning land developers, real estate brokers, attorneys, and others with vested interests in commerce that may come before the Board or Council. Your responsibilities may include approving annexations, land contracts, zoning changes, road contracts and service agreements.

As a rule of thumb, keep most donations small and somewhat equal in size, unless you truly know what the motivation is. If Aunt Millie wants to give you a $1,000 its probably safe to assume she truly wants to help her nephew. On the other hand if Millie works for the local Land Baron you may have to question

Millie's intentions before accepting. But if everyone from Millie to the big land developer is only giving you $50, no one could ever claim you have sold out to big business, or Aunt Millie. When you are seeking smaller rather than larger donations, you may have to work harder to encourage and secure the funding but you will be beyond reproach from the public, the press, and your opponents. Opponents may seek out your campaign finance filings, which are public records, and question donations made by certain people. If this happens, you have to go on the defensive wasting precious time trying to defend yourself. If donations fall into the same general amount, you have a solid defense pointing out that Aunt Millie and Donald Trump gave you the same amount.

Also try to keep financial filings handy at all times to show to the press if you have to, to knock down questions and unstated innuendo before they get out of hand. In most campaigns no one will question your integrity, but every now and then, a campaign will get nasty and some opponent or campaign manager will look into your financial dealings looking for an edge.

Please don't think that running for public office is such a dirty, backbiting business that you won't want to continue. It is actually just the opposite; it is a wonderful experience that goes quite well 99.7% of the time. But every now and then you will have someone who may try to cause problems, and that is one of the reasons I wrote the book. For your first campaign effort you may be shy and not want to ask for money to help defray costs. There is nothing wrong with that and you can fund the campaign entirely by yourself, but it only empties your own pocket. Let your friends and relatives help out. They will do so willingly and get a kick out of being a part of a campaign. The secret is don't ask anyone for a lot, instead ask for small donations (in check form, made out to your campaign fund) and you will have all sorts of donors.

In-kind donations were mentioned before and it is important that you understand that all value given to you for the campaign must be recorded to keep everything above board and in front of the public's eye. That includes someone volunteering their copier at work to make copies of your handout brochures, or a good writer friend offering to write that spellbinding campaign speech for you. It includes the lumber guy on the edge of town donating two hundred stakes for your yard signs, and the bar owner throwing in a free keg of beer at your fundraiser. You can and should accept all of these in-kind gifts if you want to, but they should be recorded on the financial reports that must be filed with the State, so that they are out in the open for all to see. It is for your protection and the person making the donation.

When you are donating to your own campaign fund, don't just use cash out of your pocket, or write a check directly to a vendor. Instead write the check to your own campaign fund checking account, and then use those candidate account checks made out in the name of the "Campaign Fund for XXX" to pay for the service or materials you are purchasing. You are trying to lay down a very clear paper trail that shows where all the money has come from and where it is going. Do these things and you won't have the state breathing down your neck, and you take a potential problem out of the hands of your opponents.

Developing Campaign Literature

Using the term literature for campaign materials might be stretching the truth a bit, but the fact remains that you need something to tell the public who you are, what you believe in, and why they should vote for you. So you need at least one well thought out, easy to read brochure, which can be shared with people as you work your way through the neighborhoods. You need to develop a message that reflects what you believe in, suggests why you're the person to represent the voters interests, and what your background is all about to gain the voters confidence that you can do the job. And all this should be wrapped up in a nice tight little presentation that is simple to read and makes the voters want to vote for you.

Today, these brochures can be made quite efficiently on a home computer and even customized for different audiences to better sell the candidate. The key to designing a good piece is to keep it simple and pleasing to the eye. Keep in mind that if you can actually get someone to look at the document you have about three seconds to grab their attention before they put it down and forget about what your pitching. I usually design a number of different pieces all using the same basic information but arranged somewhat differently to meet specific agendas, needs and audiences.

The key is to design a piece that is versatile, that can be used early in a campaign when you are going door-to-door, could be handed out at a political rally or speaking engagement, and then used later as a mailing for that last minute blitz. Years ago, when you still needed to send out for typesetting, photo screening and readable font options, I decided to design a mini-newsletter for the district I was running in. I had determined early on that the incumbent was not communicating with his constituents and that this lack of communication was a sore point with the voters.

In that election, the time was ripe to send a newsletter to show I could communicate. In the first issue, which was hand delivered by me and my Committee during the campaign itself, I promised to send a quarterly newsletter like this to keep everyone aware of what was going on if I got elected. It got me noticed quickly because I had found a way to capture their attention, something the incumbent was not doing.

While I did not have an insider viewpoint on all the issues, I developed some issue summaries from the local newspapers and then offered my viewpoint. I also added all sorts of helpful information about street repair, snowplowing, trash pick-ups, emergency call numbers, phone numbers of various city departments and such that I had gleaned from other sources. When the first issue was hand delivered to the 5,000 residents, I was up and running.

My candidacy all of a sudden had wings and visibility. The local press took note and asked why I had decided to take this approach. I responded by saying my research had shown my constituents felt they needed more communication and I intended to offer it. The campaign piece I designed even looked like a small newspaper with various headlines and articles that all started on the front page and jumped inside. It was inexpensive to print, and had the legs to be used throughout the campaign. I attribute my victory to this newsletter because it was the right approach at the right time.

Part of that success was due to the fact that I had spoken to a good number of citizens and determined that there was a good amount of dissatisfaction with the incumbent. I decided to jump on that underlying dissatisfaction and be pro-active offering just what was lacking.

If you chose such an approach for your campaign you don't have to spend a lot of money and make it a real dynamic form. With today's computers you should be able to whip up a Newsletter in no time at all. Your presentation for-mat should be a simple, well-delivered message that caters to the interests of the voters. You need to talk to the people to find out what is on their minds and what they believe the issues to be. It is also presents a great communication opportu-nity to ask some survey questions, and solicit a response from the citizens. By tying such a survey to your campaign website you can drive people to another campaign promotion opportunity, where they can find out more about you. Everything should be tied together. You want to lead potential voters to even more information about you. You want them to feel as if they know you and that you can be trusted with their vote.

The All-Purpose Brochure

When designing an all-purpose brochure, one that can be used in a variety of situations, you definitely want to include your picture and possibly a photo of your family to convey that you are a family oriented individual. There should be a short personal message, in a sentence or two, telling the voters why you are running. Then you should ask them to consider you as a candidate. And that is in the first few lines of copy.

Once you have established you are running and would like their vote, you should discuss some of the current issues facing the elected body and position yourself accordingly. You need to take a stand on the issues. Declare you are for or against them but don't waffle. People want and need to know where you stand and it is to your advantage to tell them, even if it may not be what some of them want to hear.

Over the years I have developed many different brochure formats, but if I were to recommend one universal type it would be on 81/2" x 11" paper stock designed to be a tri-folded document. You can get a good idea of options available by going to www.paperdirect.com; www.imageshoponline.com; www.designerpapers.com. Paper Direct is a specialty paper company out of Colorado Springs, CO., Phone: 800-272-7377. The company offers all sorts of plain and colored papers that can be used for brochures. In their catalog they have a whole section on Brochure paper in double fold, tri-fold and others in a variety of weights and styles. It is worth visiting the site just for ideas. Much of this paper can be ordered direct to your home and used on your own PC to produce first class brochures that will allow you to stand out in a crowd of competitors using white paper stock. While the paper is a bit more costly, usually sold in lots of 100, it can be well worth it because printing the color on your own can be even more costly.

In recent years the major office supply stores like Office Max and Office Depot all carry pre-printed specialty papers that have been designed for brochure use. There is an even greater selection of pre-printed colored paper stock available in the major office supply store catalogs. You can also find such stock in small print stores and special printing shops, although they will want you to do the design work through them in order to order the stock.

The nice part about these specialty papers is that there are a huge variety of color designs available, many with color that would otherwise be very expensive to have printed in a traditional quick printer mode on white paper. Check out the designs that are available in the shops and ask your printer what types of specialty paper they may have available as well. The designs and color make it look like you have something special that a voter needs to look at. Remember you have about three seconds to make a good impression, so good paper stock might get them to take a look.

You want to find a design that will enhance your message without overpowering it. Have you ever received a note on paper stock that had so much going on that you had a hard time deciphering the actual message? You don't want to confuse the voter. You just want to give him something that looks good enough to investigate further. You want something that will enhance your message. I stay away from stock that has American Flags on the borders, or has some other very busy design. I try to find a design that has a two-tone effect as background that will almost frame the message I place within it.

Your local quick printer can provide you with all sorts of ideas and options but some of them can be pricey. If cost is not a concern (because you have a cracker jack Finance Committee) then you should work with a local quick printer. He has access to all the pre-printed paper stock and could make recommendations. Keep in mind that he will want to sell you the bulk paper and print it for you once the message is crafted. Let the printer know what you are trying to accomplish, what kind of piece counts and volumes you are looking for, and what kind of budget you have to work with. He can offer all sorts of ideas on how to attain great results. Make him a partner in your campaign. As a small businessman in your district he will enjoy being apart of the campaign and will support you.

I had one printer who showed me how to utilize fluorescent orange card stock to make a 5 ½" by 8" inch hand-outs that looked like a miniature Renk yard sign on the fluorescent side and had campaign information on the other. We actually used my Yard sign design on the fluorescent side. Because it was heavy duty, bright cardstock, it stood up well, and as I handed them out going door-to-door, I encouraged voters to put the miniature sign in their front windows (to ward off other candidates, which was a joke but many people liked the idea).

I would have never thought about the concept but the printer offered a great suggestion and got a great little printing order out of the recommendation. Your printer knows how to use paper, how it folds depending on thickness, how it takes ink, and what a photograph will look like on certain papers. Trust your printer's insights and use his best judgment when designing a piece. Tell him what you are trying to accomplish and he will offer all sorts of ideas. He probably has dozens of past political brochures tucked away in some file drawer that would offer all sorts of ideas. Ask for suggestions on how to design a universal campaign piece that can be used door-to-door, can be distributed in the mail, can be used at events, and left as a calling card when no one is home.

By creating a universal piece you may only have to design one brochure, print one large run of copies, and in doing so, save a bunch of money. Good planning is the key. If you know someone who designs publications, publishes books or works for a newspaper, see if you can get them on your committee. They could offer valuable insights as well.

Then sit down with your committee and design this piece to be useful in all sorts of situations. In my experience that usually will mean you are looking at a tri-folded 8 ½" x 11" brochure that can carry all of the information you want and can be used in a variety of situations.

A tri-fold brochure will give you six panels to work with to convey your message. You can visualize This by simply taking any 8 ½" X 11" sheet of white paper and folding it with two folds as if it were to fit in a standard envelope. There are a number of ways to tri-fold a standard piece of paper and the way you end up doing it may change where the cover panels and mail panels will be located.

You can fold it like a typical letter is folded; inward much like a—U—shaped letter, or you can fold it in a—Z—format. Either will work but you may want to play with the two styles to see where you would put your important information and messages. Using blank paper, fold them both ways and then write out what information you would drop into each panel. Try it both ways and then using a pen, write notations on the various panels that are created. Give it a try with some blank paper and you will see what I mean.

Pencil in the following major categories on the various panels. Include:

- A Cover and Introduction photo panel
- Your Address and <u>Disclaimer</u> panel (opposite panel from Cover)
- Key Major Issues and Concerns to be presented
- Your Personal Background
- Your Schooling and Civic Credentials

That adds up to five panels and you may have even more information in mind. That's why you want to play with the layout of the document to determine what is the best information to present. Always remember that a voter's attention span while standing at the door is about three to five seconds, and half that if the wind is blowing. You need something that will grab attention.

In most states there are Disclaimer requirements that must be shown on all campaign materials. In simple terms it is a statement that you have authorized and paid for this document to be created and distributed. It is a requirement that makes you stand by what you say, print, authorize and distribute. In some cases it can be as simple as "Paid for by (candidate)", or "authorized and paid for by the (Candidate) Campaign Committee".

Some states require the Candidates name, the Committee, a street address, to be placed in a conspicuous place and easily seen. This disclaimer works to protect you so that some scurrilous campaign brochure (by a third party) cannot be distributed in your name. The disclaimer presumption is that you personally stand by what is stated or said. A verbal variation of this disclaimer can also be found in radio and television ads where the candidate himself may have recorded a disclaimer saying "I'm George Bush and I paid for this Ad".

In some States the disclaimer rules may not apply to certain campaign articles and promotion items because they would be so small they would be impossible to read and thus would have no real purpose. Examples of these items would be badges, balloons, buttons, key tags, pencils, rulers, and a host of other small promotional products. If in doubt ask someone with local knowledge of the laws in your state. Suffice it to say that a disclaimer is an important part of all your campaign literature and must be given a prominent location on all the pieces.

If you intend to spend a good amount of effort stating the case for your important issues, then use two of the inside center panels to do a spread. The key is to see how the brochure will open up and be presented to the voters. You want it to flow nicely, look professional, and convey the important information to grab the voter's interest.

Keep in mind that the voter when first receiving this document may only casually look at it and will definitely not read it cover to cover savoring every word that you have written. You want to design the piece so it catches the eye and draws the potential reader to look further into the document. That is why photos are used so effectively in magazines on the newsstands. As an example think how many people look at only the National Geographic photos and not the copy, although the writing is terrific.

With your brochure copy, always try to simplify the words and sentences down to short bullet point phrases rather than long narrative paragraphs. Rather than a lengthy narrative, say things like:

- **Seeking** Retail & Commercial to diversify tax base
- **Endorses** New Park District Land Purchase
- **Determined** to limit Airport Expansion
- **Adamantly Opposed** to costlier Garbage Contract

No one will read long paragraphs, (except maybe your spouse, and then only because you ask them to proof it). Always try to create simple design, lots of white space and easy to read bullet points, using action verbs because you need to have the voter identify with you in about three to five seconds.

Once you have a feel for how the document should open up and be viewed, then start thinking about what to actually say. When your ready to write the copy that will go into these brochure panels, don't think of them as small chunks of information that need to be squeezed into a three by four inch panel. Instead, put the brochure design aside and work with separate new sheets of paper to type up everything that you believe in and want to address in the brochure. Don't worry about limiting your thoughts to a few inches of space. Just get all of your thoughts and concerns down on paper. A by-product of this exercise is that you will begin to build your positions on the issues for the campaign.

Then you can start to refine these words, streamlining the copy down to the important ideas you want to convey. Once you start summarizing and simplifying what you have written, you will be able to craft some bullet points. You will find that bullet points work even better because you get the voters to think about how they feel about a subject with a quick scan of the brochure.

In my experience of ringing doorbells and handing out all sorts of political brochures, less copy is better because most people will not read all the beautiful words you have written. Use bullet points to feature key topics and are of concern to you. When a voter looks at the brochure, they may ask what you think about a subject and you then have an opportunity to engage in a direct conversation and perhaps earn their vote.

Once you have the copy you like, put it aside and look at it again the next day when you are fresh. Look at it as a casual voter would. In fact, find a casual voter in your household, (perhaps your spouse could make believe she is a casual voter for a moment), or go next door, and ask for the neighbors' opinion.

Here's what voters should see in the copy:

- Does the brochure introduce YOU the candidate?
- Does it explain what YOUR interests are?
- Does it show YOU have the desire to run?
- Does it show YOU care about the community?
- Does it show YOU have experience?
- Does it encourage the voter to ask YOU a question?

All these questions and answers should be rolled into the document. Armed with the casual voter's feedback, go back to the drawing board and refine the document even more. The secret is to get as many outside opinions as you can before you print the document, because afterwards you will have wasted a lot of money if you need to change it. You need other people's opinions because it brings a fresh perspective to something you are already very close to.

Before printing expand the review circle one more time and show the draft document to your committee members and family. Ask them to be critical and look at the brochure as if they were casual citizens that had to get up from watching a football game on TV to answer the door. Take good notes on their comments, as first impressions will be invaluable, just as a citizen at the door would have, once you are ringing doorbells.

Once you have all the background prepared, reviewed and refined then its time to actually load it into the brochure template. The tri-fold paper should be carefully analyzed as you assemble each component piece because the panels all must be in specific locations for the printing and folding process. This must also jive with the actual presentation plans. That is, will the cover panel lead to the major issues and then lead to the personal information panel, etc? If you will be mailing the document you want to have a mail/address panel available as well. Good design will allow you to use the one piece of campaign literature in a number of ways, and save you money.

On that Cover panel you want to announce what office you are running for, and I recommend that this also be where you locate your standard head and shoulders photograph. (You should have the shot done professionally as you may need it for other press functions). A color photo is best but if you are having the overall document quick printed it will add considerable cost due to the more complicated printing process. If you are doing low volume, you may be able to use a computer laser color printer to get a good resolution image but this can be costly with any volume. Such documents can be quick copied at stores like Kinko's and other quick printers. If you buy the paper and a replacement cartridge, perhaps your employer would be willing to let you run the color copies on the copier or printer at work. A black and white photo can work just as well as long as it is a good resolution photo that is lit correctly because in the printing process, much of the detail will be lost.

Next, you should turn the brochure master over to find which panel is opposite your cover/photo. This should be designated as the self-mailer panel, (designing it as a self-mailer will save you the cost of envelopes and stuffing them). This panel should be left open for mailing labels and note writing, which I will talk more about later. Please note that depending on how the document is being folded, this panel may need to be upside down from the others when the document is laid out flat, but that is not a problem once it is folded for delivery. A printer can help you visualize how the document folds and opens correctly.

On this self-mailer panel you should also put your return address, phone, and e-mail information and website so voters could contact you if they wished to do so. This is also a good location to put any required Campaign Fund disclaimers about who has authorized and paid for the printing. This information is often required by state election law and must be on every piece of literature that you develop. Thus it should be placed on the master that will be printed, otherwise you might have to create an ink stamp with the disclaimer, and stamp each piece to conform to state law. (Been there, done that).

This is also the panel where I would display the Union "bug" label if the document is to be printed in a union shop. Many union people will look for the union shop label and ask if a non-union print shop did the printing. Your print shop will be happy to put the union bug on the piece if they are union. I will talk more about the union "bug" later.

That leaves you four panels to cover your issues, background, hopes for the district and other things you deem important. I would recommend that you think about breaking all this copy up with another photograph or two. This could be where you show that you are a family person, and it could be where you show yourself going door-to-door, even if it's a photo of you walking up to your own front door. It conveys a message.

Photos are Worth a 1,000 Words

Most people remember that dramatic photo of the Chinese student standing in front of the military tanks preventing them from moving in Tiananmen Square in Beijing in the mid-90's. Good photos tell a story.

Campaigning for public office is another situation where good pictures can do a world of good for you. Photographs are important because the general public has no idea who you are or why they should vote for you. That's why Hollywood stars have publicists, to keep their client's names and photo's in front of the publics' eyes. In this same manner, you need to put a face with your name and you need to humanize yourself so they are thinking of you as person, someone they could care about.

In an early campaign, I was shameless and used a photo of myself holding my baby daughter, and she was a beautiful little child. As you might guess, when I handed out the brochure everyone commented on the baby and it gave me a chance to get a few words in before they lost interest and the door closed. Photos create visual interest.

That's why you should always pay attention to the photos you include in the campaign information. If running for a Fire Commission position, try to get a photo with fire personnel next to a fire truck. Visit the Chief and ask him to allow such a photo shoot. If running for the water or sewage commission, stand next to the water filtration or sewage processing plant. If running for School Board show yourself at a school event or with children in front of a school bus to convey an image that says your already in the game!

The movie stars in Hollywood make a big deal out of being at the Oscars even though only a few of them actually receive honors. If I were the incumbent, I would include a photo of me sitting at my council chamber desk with my Name card in front of me. It conveys that I already have earned the seat and should be retained. If I were challenging the incumbent, I would have my picture taken standing next to the Village Hall sign, or even better, at the Public Works building standing next to a village snowplow. Such a photo would convey a sense of linkage with the community in the mind of the voter.

You should think about how you want the voters to think of you and create a situation where you have the photo to support that image. I am a big believer in going door-to-door because it allows you to come in direct contact with every voter, or at least show them that you stopped by their home. It would tell the voters that you are making the effort. Stage a photo of you walking up to a house, or better yet a photo from the voters perspective shot through the door looking at you saying hello. This is a trickier shot to obtain because the bright outdoor light is often behind you and your face becomes a shadow. That is not what you want. This is the type of photo either a professional should light from inside, shining out, or that you could attempt with extra lighting aimed out the door to lighten up your face. This approach allows you to look at the camera as if it was a voter and smile which is another important image to leave with the voters.

Another photo may relate to a specific issue. Perhaps there is a dilapidated lot that is being considered for a park or a tot lot. Get out there and have your picture taken with kids playing in the area to convey that you support the tot lot. If there is a dangerous traffic intersection that needs a sign or stoplight, have your picture taken on the corner, with four cars in the intersection, even if you have to stage it with friends. You want to show the public that you are involved in the issues they are concerned about.

If you are a tradesman in a working class town you want to convey that you are just like the voters of that community. Have a photo of you at the worksite in a hardhat, or in the factory. But that would not be a strong image to project if your constituency is largely white-collar workers, or all suburbanites because they won't identify with you. If the white-collar crowd were your voter population you want to convey as much similarity as possible, so you should probably have a suit on and be talking to another professional person.

If you are a teacher its important to have a picture with kids to relate that you are already assisting the community in the education field. If you are a soccer mom seeking office let everyone know you are involved in your community by showing yourself with the team, because all the other soccer moms will hopefully assimilate with your experience and vote for you. If you are looking for a strong family turnout, you may want to have your whole family line up for a photo, or you may want to have a photo of you speaking at a school function with kids and parents in view.

If your community has an esteemed member of the community or a public official that is supporting you, think about a photo op with that person. I happen to live in the Congressional District where Speaker of the House, Congressman Dennis Hastert resides. All of the local politicians around here value having their picture taken with Denny, who has always been a good friend of our small communities. A picture with Denny infers you may have the ear of the gentleman third in line for the U.S. Presidency. Whenever he is in the area, he is sure to draw the local politicians for a photo opportunity for the next election. I have one and use it when I'm running for office.

But not all politicians can help your campaign. Sometimes they could be an embarrassment or a burden to have on your side. In a situation like that you are better off not making the connection.

In the 2004 Presidential election, Vice President Al Gore didn't encourage Bill Clinton to become involved in his Presidential campaign. That was perhaps because Bill brought some extra baggage with him and it would divert attention from the message that Al was trying to present. Ironically, Al Gore did not do very well on the campaign trail by himself and eventually tried to benefit from Clinton's help, but the request was a bit late in coming and as such Bill Clinton's coattails weren't strong enough to win the day.

Having a photograph with an existing politician can work for you, or it could work against you, so your Campaign Committee should give the idea some careful and objective thought as well. It is best to have clear heads consider all the ramifications of any photo's that might be used so you don't create a problem.

Another whole concept to consider is when a photo is misused to cast a candidate in a bad light. Recently I saw a candidate use rather unflattering photos of a woman opponent running for state office. It must have been a very bad hair and no make-up day because the woman came across as in need of some serious help and rest. Without even stating that the woman was too old the photo did it for the candidate.

I have also seen unscrupulous use of a photo by an opponent who using electronic manipulation inserted a candidate into a photograph that was rather compromising. Again think of a situation where you are shown coming out of the local strip club. That could cost you hundreds of votes and once such a photo was out would take on a life of its own. In the 80's former Senator Gary Hart had a picture of his mistress sitting on his lap next to a large yacht. It cost him his Presidential campaign.

Always control your photo images and let your photograph tell a positive story for you. The idea is to use the photos to convey a strong image the voters can embrace and connect with. Remember a photograph is worth a thousand words, and very few people want to read that much.

Develop a Campaign Website

While you are designing your campaign pieces you should also give considerable thought to designing a campaign website that will mirror the presentation you have in the brochure. The site can then be used to encourage all sorts of interaction and communication. And you may find that you are the only candidate that has such a site giving you an edge in gaining visibility and voter interest.

On a custom website designed for your campaign you can introduce yourself, develop your campaign themes and issues, offer background information on your career work, your community involvements and your goals for the community to each person that you can get to it. You can show the voters where you stand on controversial issues and hopefully win them over with well thought out position statement. You can show voters multiple photographs to become even more visible with them, and you can keep them updated on the campaign's progress, future events and how to go about getting registered, voting absentee or getting a lift to the polling place on election day. Think of it as your electronic brochure.

A good website can be developed just for the campaign or can be expanded to become your permanent website once the campaign has been won. Websites don't have to be expensive and technological as much as they need to be informational, completely factual, and easy to navigate. That's where a technology committee member comes in. Sites can be developed for a few hundred dollars but should provide excellent content to be truly useful. Developing website content is another job for the Committee to define issues and prepare strong position statements on them. You want to tell your story and have voters visit and come away with a desire to vote for you.

Visit any website on the web and you will see all sorts of flash and dash, but that won't necessarily earn you votes. Make your site user-friendly, easy to navigate and most important, make it interactive. It should be used to instruct voters in what you believe in and why you believe it. A personal campaign site can clearly show your positions on issues and really delve into why you have taken various positions.

By interactive I mean getting your visitors to interact with the site and your position on issues, by asking for more information or follow-up. After you state your position on an issue, ask for the visitors input. Ask them a short survey questionnaire that they could fire back to you. In that manner you will be able to build an e-mail contact list and that will allow you another way to interact with your voters. Consider adding a survey on your site that encourages voters to express views and offer their opinions. There is a service you can get off the Internet at www.pollhost.com that will allow you to add simple surveys and questions to your site. This will allow you to gather voter insights on issues and will allow you to capture voter e-mails for future use and follow-up.

Having such response interactivity you are showing voters you care about what they have to say on political issues. More importantly you are capturing their e-mail address for future use. Since they have e-mailed you, you have every right to go back to them and try to sell your candidacy Because they originally contacted you it will not be considered unsolicited SPAM. But with today's laws limiting unsolicited mail you need to be careful so that you don't turn off a voter. You want to maintain a positive relationship. Most voters will like the ability to think they can talk with a candidate

Offer the voters access to your electronic newsletter or list of campaign coffee locations by having them sign up for it, again securing an e-mail address. As you build this interactivity you will develop a list of interested voters who can be asked to help make a donation or put up a sign.

Once you have a basic website you need to keep it as up to date as you can and that means having access to make changes. Websites used to be mysterious but now almost anyone can maintain them and upgrade and change them as needed. If that isn't going to be you find someone that can deal with the technical aspects of the site for you. In most cases it will be someone under 25 and probably under 18.

You want to be able to be flexible with the site to use it as an effective campaign tool. You can add new speaking dates to invite additional voters to hear you. You want to list where coffees will be held and where people can go to register, cast an absentee ballot and find the polling places.

With a good site you then need to drive people to it by listing the website address on all your literature, signs and handouts. Every time you ring a doorbell you should ask them to visit the site to stay up to date on campaign issues and activities. More and more people are exploring websites each day and if you have a good one, people will look it over before they vote.

Campaign Sign Design

The next subject is an important one because you are probably starting from the position of being unknown with the exception of your spouse, the neighbor kids who play at your house all day long, and the guy next door who borrows all your tools. You need some basic visible name recognition so voters will know whom to check off in the voting booth. So how do you get name recognition and visibility?

Well, you are already creating a brochure that will tell people who you are and what you stand for. That's a good start, as long as you have a means to put it in peoples' hands. But you need more, you need greater visibility, so that voters will recognize your name and identify with it. You need lawn signs, or as they are often called, "yard signs". Yard signs are pretty much like real estate for sale signs in the fronts of peoples' homes all over the neighborhoods. Except these signs will proclaim your candidacy. The signs tend to be rather obnoxious and gaudy, and can be an eyesore, but they are a necessary evil you will have to consider if your opponents are using them.

By the way, if your opponents should come to you and say they have all agreed that signs aren't needed for the campaign, as they are ugly and costly, don't readily agree that you will not put any signs up. What they aren't saying is they already have enough name recognition and they don't want you to receive any exposure. Plus they are just trying to save money at your expense. Incumbents will often suggest this to a new challenger because they already have voter name recognition. When you run into this situation tell them you have already pre-ordered 500 signs because you have commitments for 200 locations already. Then stand back and watch them soil their pants. You need the exposure so don't pre-agree to an opponent's suggestions about not signing, because they are being self-serving to their campaign.

Signs are an important way of getting your name out in front of the public, stating that you are a viable candidate. Signs can make or break a campaign and must be factored into the budget early on if you truly want to gain exposure.

There are many different types of signs that can be designed and they can be designed to carry whatever message you want them to. They can be large or small, simple or complex; all determined by what you can afford to spend. And believe me, you can spend a bunch if you want to.

In early campaigns, I made some of my signs, and had help from my daughter. Homemade signs can be very effective in some political campaigns especially if you are portraying yourself as a hometown, rookie candidate, who is not just another slick politician. But if you are up against multiple candidates or deep campaign pockets, you must fight fire with fire and you will need a good number of signs to meet the challenge.

Most business sign companies can make political signs, but they can be costly. During campaign cycles, there are specialty political advertising companies that are available to make custom designed signs. The secret is to find them. Once you have they will then find you every two or four years as you will have been on the political lists and may be a potential client.

One such company is POLITICAL U.S.A. Co. in Harris, NY. 1-800-883-3662, and there are many others, probably right in your area. They offer all sorts of campaign aids and signs for large and small contests, all custom designed with your specifications in 3-5 days if you need them that fast. They can offer outside posters, pole signs, banners, buttons, bumper stickers fans, magnet signs, pens, memo pads, key chains, car signs and more. Call them for a catalog and you will see that they have it all. This is also a great way to get some estimates on costs of all these items.

In Illinois we have another company called PRC, the Political Resource Center with various franchisees taking orders on your behalf, then forwarding the orders to a bigger sign printer for processing. These middlemen companies are convenient and expedite the orders for you, and to you. They can be reached at 1-800-433-2730. there will be similar companies in your area. You just need to find them. Do a Google search for "political signs" in your area and you will find all sorts of options. The last time I did a search for "political signs" I discovered over 700,000 referrals that offer some sort of sign assistance. Also talk to any existing politician and ask them if they kept their last campaign catalog. That way you will have a contact number and you can call for current year catalog pricing.

Signs can be designed as large or small as you might want and will determine the cost factors involved. Things that you will need to consider include: the size, mounting equipment, colors, complexity versus simplicity of what you are trying to accomplish, and volume to be printed. Lets talk a little about each of those components.

Size Does Matter!

This is one of those important situations where size does matter! You have to figure that the sign placed in a front yard must be seen from the road as that is its primary purpose, to get the name recognition from those driving by. The positioning could be anywhere from 10 feet to 100 feet from the road and needs to be seen clearly to be effective. Bigger is probably better especially if you have a long last name. RENK always fit pretty well on any style of sign but when you are a Derezinkowski, you will have to compromise on the font size just to fit the name on the sign.

You can buy extra wide signs but they come at a premium cost and then the wire stanchions are more costly as well. When you have a long name you might want to think about making the sign vertical which could be mounted on a single wooden stake. Another possibility might be to place the long last name on a diagonal from top left to bottom right and simply put the words "Elect" and the office desired in the opposite upper and lower corners. I believe in simplicity, as the casual drive by glance will offer at most a second to notice the sign. Always go for the surname recognition. Skip all the secondary stuff like large first and middle names, full office title, city, village, etc., as the voters are not interested in all that clutter. They want to know that your name is on the ballot and that's it. So design your signs to be simple and easily read from a great distance. In farming communities and on major highways, drivers are shooting by at high speed and have at most a second to even notice your sign. Make it big enough to see from a distance.

In a past election four years ago, one of the other candidates went to an even higher profile on the major highway/cornfield routes. Because of state highway setback requirements set by the Highway Commission and the community, signs had to be over 50 ft back from the road. One Village Trustee decided his signs needed to be really big in these areas. So he went to the lumberyard and bought two large 4 ft. by 8 ft.' ½ inch thick panels, and cut them in half creating two 4'x 4'potential signs. He then used large stencils to hand paint: "Vote Geary" on both sides of the sign using outdoor paint in his normal sign colors. He drilled 4 small holes along each side and then bought metal stakes, the kind used to hold up road fencing. He mounted the signs with plastic tie downs 4 feet off the ground. Even from 150 plus feet off the roadway the printing size was large and clear and easily read. The signs cost him a bit more but he got 8 large signs for about $75. He also won his election. For my next election two years later he gave the signs to me and I painted his name out and put my name on them, and used the large signs in the same locations. I won the election too.

Primary Colors!

The next sign design issue is the color, or colors, that are to be used. Again, you don't need to get fancy with a lot of color because your primary goal is to leave a quick impression with the voter. If you have more than one color you may confuse the voters as they get mixed up with which candidates have which colors. Color is important if for no other reason it will distinguish you from the other candidates. Whether your name is on a matchbook, a lawn sign, a car-top carrier, a banner or a brochure, your name should always be presented in the same style and color. Its almost like creating a brand, like Coca-Cola, or Target.

Before settling on a color, ask around and see if you can find out what colors the other candidates are using. Come right out and ask them because they will not want you to use their color either. An incumbent will probably use the same colors he or she used in prior elections because there will be left over signs still useful.

Always remember, the casual drive by glance of a voter may only pick up the color, and if your opponent has the same color as you, the voter may not be able to see the name clearly and may assume the sign belongs to the other candidate.

If your opponent's color or colors can be pre-determined, then go with a different primary color. Primary colors are important because they will be seen better and from a greater distance. If you are in the Snow Belt, a fall election or a spring race could be in a blanket of snow, three feet high. You will want a color that will look bright and sharp on that snow bank. If you are running in the summer, you probably won't want green as your color, as it will blend into the green lawns. Orange may not work in the fall when the leaves are falling. And you don't want to make such color determinations after you spent $500 dollars on a sign color that will be lost in the blowing leaves. Just think ahead and pick a striking color that will be vibrant in the actual season the signs will be up. Once you decide on a color check one more time with other candidates before ordering your signs to make sure they haven't changed their color choice. (It has happened to me). If they have changed their minds again, find a different color, or you will confuse voters and yourself when you are driving around checking to see if signs are still standing.

Some sign companies will offer pre-printed sign formats that have larger and smaller type styles, two-tone colors, or American Flag/stars and stripes backgrounds in multiple colors, but all they will do is jack up the cost because of the color additions, and perhaps make them harder to read at a distance. You want to identify with the voters, so keep it simple.

Now back to design. Keep it as simple as you can, or no one will be able to read all the words and type on the sign and you will have just wasted hundreds of dollars. Make a mockup sample the size you are planning on using and stick it in your yard. Then take a walk or drive down the block and see how legible the words are from that distance. You will be surprised at how everything blends together and all you see is a color. I usually put my name as big as I can get it in standard block letter type. And I don't try to use script or cute fonts as they take away from the dynamic of projecting a good strong image a good distance.

With a smaller font add elect or re-elect as the case may be, and then simply the office being sought. Keeping the sign simple makes it more visually stimulating and voters can identify with it. Voters will recognize the sign design and color, and when they are spread all over town you gain the name recognition you so sorely need. While signs can be a real headache, they are critical marketing tools that give you fast recognition and visibility.

What's a Union Bug?

There is another thing you should ask about when you are getting your sign printing estimates. Ask the printer whether the sign shop actually doing the printing is a union shop. If they are not union, think about finding a print shop that is. Let me explain why it could be a factor in your campaign.

If the print shop is a union shop they will automatically put the union label, or "bug" as it is often called, on the signs or brochures as they are printed. This is done as a way of signing their work products, as they are proud of their union work and label. It tells the world that you have supported union labor. Have you ever driven by a building work site where there are pickets set up telling people that non-union labor is being used? It can cripple the work site or make people shy away from supporting the site.

The union issues and the so-called bug symbol could be a factor in your election too. This is especially important if you are running for office in a union town or a working class neighborhood. When you are campaigning door-to-door, union workers may ask you if you support union laborers, or your opponent might suggest that you didn't use a union shop and you can't be trusted to support union folks. Always be aware of such things because your opponent could make it an issue. Also, when you are out campaigning, a union homeowner/voter may ask where you stand on union issues. Point out the sign and the union bug on your printed brochures and they should be satisfied that you are aware that union people look out for one another.

If you are in a small town where unions are not well organized this issue may not be a factor at all, but it is worth noting so that a labor issue does not sandbag your campaign. Ask the printers you are talking to whether they are union shops. If they are union shops they know why you are asking, and will gladly make sure the bug is displayed.

If printing shops are not union organized in your area, it probably won't ever materialize as an issue. You can again get some guidance on this question by asking other current politicians, or asking your political party leaders. They can offer direction and insight and can direct you to known union shops for printing support. It is not a big deal but it could cause a campaign problem if it becomes an issue and you already printed 200-yard signs and a thousand brochures without the union bug on them. Ask early on and it won't become an issue.

How Many Signs?

"Many, many more than you think you will need."

—Tom Renk

My best answer to the above question would be more than you would ever think you will need, but this is one of those questions that only you, God and your campaign finance person will be able to truly answer. Signs are one of the most important marketing tools you will have in your arsenal. But the costs add up quickly too.

You can approach the question of how many signs you will need from a number of different directions, but you should do some serious estimating based on a number of factors. The variables can be hard to determine but if you ask yourself and your committee the following questions you should be able to come up with some good numbers. And then I would say add another 20%.

The most important question will be what is your opponent(s) doing? If they are using signs you have to respond in kind. That is why you need to ask those questions about sign colors, campaign plans, and such, so that you get an idea of what they are planning to do. With luck, they will say they are ordering 300 signs, or 50 signs, or none at all. If any candidates are ordering signs then you need to think about it as well. And you should probably order more signs than your opponent, because more signs will offer you more exposure, presuming you can find a site to set them up.

If you are challenging an incumbent, you will want signs regardless of whether he or she is ordering them. The incumbent already has name recognition and exposure and may be a local community celebrity. You on the other hand have no name recognition and very little community exposure, so you need to have your name out in front of the public. I would order a good number of signs to play catch-up

Signs are expensive. When you add up the costs of design, printing, stakes or metal rods, shipping, and distribution, the signs will easily cost over $4.00–5.00 each in today's dollars. When you do the math, 300 signs can cost a good amount of your total budget. But they are probably the best exposure you can get for the money. If I have to stretch anywhere, it will be with my signs, because it offers the greatest visibility benefit right up to the election.

In a small community, 50 well placed signs might be all the attention you need. And good locations for the signs are very important. In a small town you want them to be placed up and down Main Street, the same road everyone uses to go to the post office, the store, to school and to church. In a larger community you will need more signs because you want people to be able to see your name in all parts of town. In a community of 5,000, I once ordered only 100 double-faced signs and it was not enough by the time the election came around and people were actually paying attention to the election. But with the election just around the corner it was too late to have more printed. I lost that election!

Signs also take a beating in the elements, especially if you are running for office in the fall or winter/spring cycle. Wind alone will pull down and blow away a good number of signs, some to the next county. Snow and rain will also wreak havoc on signs, thus you need to have backups available to replace missing or torn up signs. Make sure that your printer is using a good, thicker card stock and pay the few extra cents to have the signs clear-coat sealed to ward off the elements. Signs can now be ordered that actually fold over as one piece of the card stock. This is important because that way there is no seam at the top and rain and water affect them less. Explore your sign options carefully, ask questions of printers and other candidates so that you understand what you are buying. I don't suggest skimping on signs. Put the money you have to into them as it will pay off in the long run.

Location, Location, Location!

Just like real estate, location, location, location is the most critical factor in getting good exposure and visibility with sign placement. I always look for optimum location and good sightlines. Getting good locations will pay many for itself throughout the campaign.

A political sign is meant to register visual and mental images to the potential voters. You want them to recognize your name, remember it and store it away to be called up when they are in the voting booth. The constant visual image of a sign is important for voter recognition. A voter may not remember what party you are from, what issues you stand for or even what office you are seeking, but he may remember a name he saw everyday for three weeks plastered on those red signs all over town. It is not what you would call intelligent voting, but it is a fact of political life.

If you don't go after that name recognition your opponent will. You have to remember that when the voting booth closes, the voter may or may not remember what the issues are or where you stand on them, but he might remember the image of your yard sign and relate it to your face when you visited his front door. If you had a sign on the lawn down the block from the polling place he may put it all together and remember your name. Then he pulls the lever next to your name.

Try to seek out street corner intersections because you get the benefit of cross exposure with people driving by in two different directions. Front lawns with a high hill also make great locations because the sign is prominently up there in clear view. On top of a hill it will also be away from the sidewalk traffic and kids that try out their karate kicks on the way home from school. Scout out sign locations at the entrances to sub-divisions, across from schools, at entrances to shopping areas, and in the businesses themselves. You need visibility so look to where the people are shopping, attending church, going to schools and driving to work.

Stay on the busier streets first because of the traffic potential and then move into interior neighborhoods. Go where the traffic patterns are.

If this is a first election, utilize any location you can obtain to start with and then as new locations are identified, if you have used all of your signs available, move your existing ones around to better locations. Take the signs that are deep in neighborhoods or on dead-end streets, and move them to heavier traffic areas as you get closer to the election. You should also concentrate signage near the schools and public buildings that will be used on election day as polling places, because you will get one last impression before voters actually show up to vote. I have even placed signs in an area outside the actual boundary lines of the jurisdiction, or outside the community, because voters saw the signs as they drove to the voting place.

Most states have regulations about how close signs can be to the polling place. You should find out what those distances are and find locations that are close but outside that prescribed distance. Presume your opponents will be looking at this as well. Over the years I have seen elections where opponents and election judges have complained about signs being too close to the polling place. The police are often called to pull up the infringing signs. But if you know the distances to the polling place door, you can have your signs legally in place all day long while people are voting. An opponent may try to have them taken down, but if you know you are within the law and legal, have a campaign worker put them back up again.

You could also have a couple of car or truck signs made that would be parked for the day outside the signage limit area. I remember one large city election when the campaign committee parked a semi-truck with a 40 x 10 foot campaign banner sign in a legal parking spot on a major bridge overpass during the morning and afternoon rush hours. Every motorist on the way to work that day passed under that bridge and large banner sign and knew it was Election Day. Then in the afternoon the truck was moved to the other side of the overpass to catch all the homebound traffic reminding voters they should still vote. That candidate won the election handily because he had great visibility and gave all the voters a large visual image just before they cast their ballots.

The key to good sign location is to be creative. Then all you have to do is secure the locations with permission from the property owners. The secret is to ask. The worst that can happen is that someone says no.

In a town with a main street, you should walk the entire street, visiting each shop with signs under your arm, introduce yourself to the proprietor, and ask if you could put a sign in the window. Many of the owners and managers will say yes. And if your opponents have already placed signs in shops, don't pass them by, rather, go in and visit with the business owner. Most business people will not want to offend you or their customers by supporting a particular candidate, so they will take your sign as well. They are interested in looking as if they support all candidates. Use that to your advantage by placing your sign right next to your opponents if need be. Think about the advantage your opponent has if you don't attempt to secure the same locations.

One final caveat, it is perhaps obvious that you don't put a sign in certain locations that could offend voters. The most obvious example is at the strip club at the edge of town, but there are also other less obvious places that you do not want your sign to be seen. If the corner gas station with the bad oil smell or the pool hall with the bad reputation for drunken brawls has signs in their windows, the signs will hurt you. If you have a sign manager make sure your instructions on placement are clear or you may find his brother-in-law putting a sign at the off-track betting parlor. You should regularly check where your signs are supposed to be to prevent one of them from being moved to some unsavory location (like a Strip Club), by an opponent, or someone with a grudge against you. Politics is fraught with danger and intrigue, so keep an eye on your campaign at all times.

Ask and You Shall Receive

To obtain good sign locations you have to ask people to allow you to put a sign up. It's that simple. And the worst they can say is No! Start looking for sign locations when you are passing your nomination papers to get on the ballot. You will find that certain people are interested in what you are trying to do. They are the ones to ask because it gives them a way to participate in the election process. The worst thing they can say is no and then there is a house right next door that may say yes. So just ask!

Look at your community maps which we have already talked about and try to identify target areas where signs will have great visibility because you have limited numbers, you have to get the most bang out of them that you can. Look for busy corners, major roads, public buildings, schools and shopping areas where people congregate. Then ring doorbells in the area with your brochure in hand and introduce yourself. If the door is opened, get a conversation going on the issues and suggest that this spot would be a great location for a sign and would they allow you to put one up?

Over the years, I've developed some personal beliefs on signage that has worked well for me. I hope my opponents are not reading this. Many candidates will put out signs as soon as they identify a location, as early as three and four months prior to the election. I don't use that approach. I am confident from my many campaigns that the public doesn't really engage the election process early in the campaign. The general public doesn't want to care about or pay attention to election issues until just before an election. Thus I think signs should be out for only a short time to maximize exposure when people are actually thinking about the election. This has worked well for me.

I line up all sorts of sign locations throughout the campaign, but tell people my signs will only be up in their front yards for about two to three weeks prior to the election. I have found that people appreciate the fact that they don't have to have a garish brightly colored sign on their lawn for months at a time. They are more willing to put up with the imposition for a few weeks. I also advise them that I will take care of the sign should it fall over or disappear, and promise that the sign will be removed right after the election. People seem to appreciate this approach. And it saves you time, money and effort in not having to keep the signs up for months.

I encourage this approach even if your opponent(s) have their signs out there much earlier. Voters aren't paying much attention to campaign issues early in a campaign. When signs are out early, voters become so accustomed to them that they look right past or through them. As the election gets closer and the election hype goes up, people begin to pay attention to what is going on. Then 17 days before the election when you put all your signs out at the same time, the visual impact will be impressive because all of a sudden you have 200 bright blue signs pop-up on street corners and in the neighborhoods all over the district. You will get noticed in a big way.

My actual sign distribution event is always scheduled on a Saturday morning. I try to line up a number of people to help with the sign effort so that the task is not too much for any one person. On that Saturday, I try to get an early morning start before most residents are even up and moving about. With good help you can put up 200–300 signs in a few hours before people start driving around on their weekend errands.

The visual impact of all these signs just appearing out of nowhere is tremendous and it is worth waiting until just two weeks before the election. Once you are close to the election, within 20 days or so, people are already aware that there is an election that will be held and they are more ready to embrace your campaign efforts. When all of a sudden they see hundreds of signs spring up overnight, you create a buzz. People who know you are pleased to see the signs are finally up, and everyone else is asking themselves who is this person.

The bottom line is you are looking for exposure and an edge. Signage can give that to you. It is a visual hook that can draw people into at least acknowledging your campaign is front and center. Use your signs for effect and you will gain the visibility and exposure you need to win.

Once you have planted all those signs in yards across the district it is important that you thank the people who have allowed you to use their front lawns.

When you place the sign in the ground, leave a short pre-printed thank you note in the homeowner's door. Besides thanking them, assure them you will take care of the sign should it get knocked down or disappear, so that they don't have to go looking for it or chasing it down the street in a windstorm. Give them your phone number, or your sign Chairman's number so they can call if the sign should disappear. Then make a promise to take it down promptly after the election. They will appreciate this and your good manners will encourage them to be sure to vote for you.

Most important, make sure you arrange to have the signs pulled down right after the election, as they can easily become an eyesore after the fact. I have been known to go out after the polls close and before results are in and pull them myself. If I have some help available, we all take various sections of town and meet up at the election party, which allows all the signs to be thrown in a truck and taken home for storage. Most of the decent signs can be used again if you bother to collect them and have a place to store them out of the weather.

By paying attention to all these details, you will earn the respect of the people who have helped you and the next time around you will already have hundreds of sign locations available to you. But still ask their permission the next time you have to run for office. If you have done a good job, they will willingly support you again.

Planting Signs in the Ground

This is an important story to save you a lot of personal wear and tear on your body and your mind. As a novice candidate 28 years ago, I was putting up signs for the very first time. On that day I almost sat down in the snow and cried.

Leading up to my sign distribution day, I had spent weeks getting the sign locations determined and the signs printed. Back then, campaign signs were usually single faced cardstock that had to be stapled back-to-back to a second sign and then both surfaces would be stapled to a wooden stake. I had dutifully purchased wooden 1" x 2'" eight foot long furring strips from the lumberyard. These were cut in half at a sharp angle to create 4 foot long sharp pointed stakes for driving into the ground. I was ready to go! Then, as the rookie candidate, I assembled all the components in my basement and stapled the signs to the boards. I created 150 sign sets and was ready to do battle. The next morning I loaded up the car and set off to my first sign location. It was very cold and there were a couple inches of snow on the ground.

I took out a sign and a small sledgehammer and attempted to pound the sign into the ground. With the first swing the wooden stake and sign completely shattered. I had forgotten that the ground was completely frozen, hard as rock. When the wooden stake shattered it also tore the affixed signs apart. So I tried again. Same result, even though I tried to hammer more lightly the second time barely even scratching the surface of the earth. I looked down at the mess at my feet and then over at my car trunk with the remaining 148 assembled signs and realized I had a serious problem. I think I would have cried except that the tears would have frozen on my face just like the ground that was denying me access. I retreated home to consider my dilemma.

I had spent hours pre-assembling the sign components and each time I tried to hammer them in, the stake shattered and the staples holding the sign were loosened enough that the sign dropped off the stake. So I realized I had to start over and took everything apart again.

150

After further testing, this time in my own back yard so that I wouldn't be so embarrassed, I determined that the only way I was going to get the signs in the frozen ground was to pre-drive a similar sized metal wedge into the earth first, to break the frozen ground. Once I had gotten about 8 inches into the earth, the stake could be driven the rest of the way to secure it. The back-to-back sign could be slipped over the wooden stake and stapled to the stick. After having wasted all the time to pre-assemble and disassemble the signs, I was back in business.

But a valuable lesson was learned and I pass it on to you. Also, by asking questions of friendly politicians and candidates who have already gone down these roads you will save yourself a lot of time and wasted energy. No one should be made to cry while standing out in the cold. The tears freeze and you really look silly! (Been there done that.)

Today signs are much more user—friendly than they used to be, and come in all sorts of sizes for different needs. You can get them large and small, as large as four feet by eight feet, and as small as business cards to hand out at meetings. A good sign shop can offer you all sorts of options, including banners that can be put on poles and strung across streets and vehicles.

Sign printers often make the signs double faced now so they can be folded over with no exposed seam on the top. That prevents signs from getting waterlogged. Then they bond the sides at the factory (for a price) so that much of the stapling is also eliminated. Instead of wooden stakes you can now buy metal rods that are bent into U-shaped forms to give the signs more stability and wind resistance. These metal stakes which are slender and sharper, seem to slide into the earth better, although you still may need a metal stake or hammer to get them through the top few inches of frozen ground. Then you just slide the signs over the top like a sock and secure it with a few staples to prevent the wind from blowing them off the stake. And you're in business.

Sign companies will also sell the same signs as one-sided signs for window use and one direction sighting. Single sided signs can be used effectively as window signs at the retail establishments where you want the image to project out onto the street. Talk with your sign guy to see what options exist. They can often sell you the whole kit including double sleeved sign and metal stakes for a package price or you can buy the components separately. Prior candidates will have metal stakes left over so they may buy the separate components.

So Where are all your Signs?

Once all your campaign signs are up, you should check them on a regular basis because of the elements and other even more sinister things that could happen while your back is turned. After your signs are up compile a Master List with specific addresses showing where all the sign locations are supposed to be. That way, you and your campaign workers can check signs on a regular basis just by doing drive-bys. You will soon be wondering why some signs are destroyed or missing so quickly. A number of things could be happening. First, there are the vandals and bored kids who see the sign as a target. Kids will be especially active on weekends when they can be out in the evenings with mischief on their minds. Kids of all ages will kick the signs down or even more maliciously actually rip them up. This is extremely frustrating because the signs easily cost $4-5 dollars each once you figure all the costs, and that is before all the manual labor and on-going maintenance goes into the effort.

Kids like to use political signs as home base for their kick-the-can game and as a soccer goal targets coming home from school. It's going to happen so be prepared with extra signs and a lot of patience. I have even seen young adults who are participating in scavenger hunts see how many signs they can collect and steal in a neighborhood. The good news is the signs usually turn up in the neighborhood intact and re-usable, all you have to do is look around to find them. The last time that happened to me, another candidate friend found 57 signs from four candidates in a front yard blocks away from where they should have been. He took his signs and called all the candidates to come and get their signs. He did it that way so people watching would not think he was the one who had taken them in the first place, or that he was trying to destroy them. Everyone appreciated his effort because each sign cost over four bucks and finances were tight.

The weather will be the biggest detriment to your signs. In the spring and fall you will get the great gale winds that rip signs right out of the ground. If you are lucky they will be found somewhere nearby under a tree or in a field, but they could be in the next county as well.

All you have to do is start a general canvas of the area and usually you will find them stuck in bushes or wrapped around the corner of another house. If you can find them you may be able to repair and use them again. You would be surprised what a little clear box wrapping tape can do to fix a sign. Remember, that people will view the sign from a distance so all the small rips; tears and tape cannot be seen from the road. But you shouldn't use a sign that is beyond repair because your host resident may be embarrassed to have such a ratty looking sign in their yard. That is why it's a good idea to order more than you think you will need, to replace all the lost and torn signs.

It's a good idea to have a complete sign repair and maintenance kit stored in the trunk of your car during the campaign so that you can repair signs on the spot. Carry extra signs, backup stakes, a hammer, staple gun and clear strong tape. Also collect torn signs to see if you can salvage them once you get home. After a while you will know where all your signs are with just a glance down the street allowing you to cruise around and make sure they are still up. A good strong single color makes that even easier to do.

Last year I ran into another mischievous act that momentarily set me back. Kids had decided to re-arrange my signs, that is, exchanging my signs with other candidate's signs. The next morning I received calls complaining they didn't want my sign and where was my opponents sign. It took a few moments to figure out what had happened but I got together with the other candidate and we unraveled the damage. If it's possible the kids will find a way to make mischief.

One other even more dire possibility for vandalism should be mentioned. Heaven forbid that you have an opponent or opponents' followers who decide to take issue with your signs and sign placement. On two occasions in 25 years of running for office and managing various campaigns, I have seen outright vandalism from an opponent's camp. This included stealing signs, trashing them in dumpsters and in one case running them over with a truck right through someone's front yard.

I'm from the Chicago area where machine politics and the comment to "vote early and vote often" is often heard, and often nasty vandalism has been a sorry part of the election trade. I have seen signs destroyed and marked with obscene words, or stolen and displayed in places that a candidate would rather not be associated with (the strip club comes to mind). If you run into this situation, first get the signs picked up, fixed or replaced, before anything else is done. I would also immediately report such problems to the police. But before you make any direct accusations, make sure you know what happened and who was specifically involved, because the press will get involved quickly, and once any accusations are made the issue will take on a life of its own.

Above all, do not fight fire with fire. Instead, take the high road and try to turn the unfortunate incident into some positive public relations for you. As soon as you stoop down to that level you will have lost the election. People will only see you doing something wrong or illegal and it will end your campaign. A quiet conversation with the opponent advising you are concerned about vandalism should give the person sufficient warning that you are taking it seriously and will not tolerate such behavior. Advise them you will call the police again if necessary. Usually you will find the police to be helpful, again, because you may become their supervisors after the election.

Door-To-Door Campaigning

"The best argument against democracy is a five minute conversation with the average voter."

—Sir Winston Churchill

Door-to-Door campaigning is the heart and soul of your election and the soles of your shoes. Door-to-Door (D-to-D) is where you get to introduce yourself to the public and hopefully make a good impression with them. Pressing the flesh is more important than all the money, friends and signs you can put up. Elections are won and lost on the amount of shoe leather a candidate is willing to wear down in a couple of months. If you are willing to pound the pavement and ring doorbells you will win the election. When candidates balk at going out to visit homes I tell them they are going to lose, especially if the other candidates are making the effort.

Going door-to-door shows the voters that you are committed to the campaign effort. To put it all in perspective, all you have to do is compute a bit of math to see what face-to-face campaigning is all about. On an average weekend campaign day from 11:00 am to 5:00 pm, about six hours, you could probably cover 150–200 homes in the suburbs, and probably double that in a more urban neighborhood. That is, walking up and down the sidewalks, ringing doorbells and introducing yourself to the homeowners who answer the door.

If you can motivate 10-20% of these individuals to vote for you, because they have personally met you and now know who you are, that is 30–50 people a day. Actually it may be double that number because spouses will often vote just like the person answering the door votes. 50+ plus people a day means 600 votes in 12 Saturdays and Sundays over the course of the campaign. That would be about three months on the campaign timeline you should have created. Most of my local campaigns were won with less than 700–1,000 votes cast. So if you ring the doorbells and introduce yourself, you can win.

When going D-to-D you can make a great first impression by using their name when you show up and say "Hello Mr. Geary". Remember, you should have cross-matched the name with the address on your polling list clipboard. Besides introducing yourself, you can usually slip in a few words while he or she is trying to figure out who you are, and how you knew their name. The voter becomes interested, if only for a few seconds, in hearing whatever pitch you want to make. You have to make the most of this first impression.

Refer to your polling list before you approach a house to see the name and look for any note that was added in your list research. It only takes a second as you approach the door. In one of my early campaigns, I must have been day-dreaming about this book because I rang the doorbell without glancing at the list and a man answered the door. I started my greeting and campaign pitch without using a name. About halfway into the pitch the gentleman smiled, held up his hand and said I should save my breath. He then stated he was glad to have met me, but that he would definitely be voting for my opponent, because he was my opponent!

I had walked up to my opponent's house without noticing the name readily highlighted on my polling list. Red-faced and rather embarrassed, I tried to save face by stumbling through my pitch. Finally, I gave up and left feeling rather foolish. In addition, I had voluntarily given up my primary campaign brochure to my opponent. Since it was early in the campaign, I had hoped that he wouldn't see it for a while so that he couldn't react to it as quickly. It was an issues and positions brochure and I'm sure that he scrutinized it to meet my challenge. I lost that race, but again learned a lesson.

When ringing doorbells you may find that the homeowners are not home. But you shouldn't consider the effort to be wasted time, it is actually just the opposite. Because you have personally visited their home you get credit for having been there even though they didn't see you. How is that so? Well, first you leave your campaign brochure in the doorframe. It tells them you stopped by to meet them. But I recommend you go even a step further and hand write a short note to them on your brochure saying something like:

"Dear Mr. Michels,

Sorry I missed you today, but I hope you will consider me when you vote Tuesday, April 1st"

Tom Renk

Then I personally sign the brochure with blue ink so the voter can see that it was really me at their door, and stick it in the door frame. I always place it in the outer screen doorframe at eye level so that they will readily see it. If there is no screen door, I will try to slide it through the inner doorframe also at eye level. In many homes the door insulation seems to allow this and the brochure is then easily seen from the outside and the inside of the house when they return. You should also keep in mind that some people rarely use their front doors anymore, because they enter and leave the home through the attached garage. If that seems to be the case, consider leaving the brochure on or near the garage door. That way the homeowners may see it before next spring.

The first time I tried this method of writing out a personalized note, I did it on the front porch of a home in 14 degree temperature. I figured the neighbors from next door were watching me to be sure I wasn't a burglar or something. After wasting a bunch of time trying to get my pen to write in the cold, I decided I had to come up with a better solution to this weather related challenge.

Now whenever I am involved in a campaign, nice and warm at home watching television, I pull up a TV table and pre-write these short "Sorry I Missed You" notes on my brochures ahead of time. I think it is important that you do this by hand and use blue ink so that the voter can truly see that you, the candidate came by, to introduce yourself.

With all my campaign brochures I always design them so there is a single panel space that can accommodate address labels, stamps and hand written notes. In this manner the brochure becomes more versatile and more useful. While I always like to add a note like this by hand, if you have the money you can have the note printed right on the brochures at the time of printing. But I would spend the money to have it done in blue ink so that it looks more like a personal note from an ink pen. The whole premise is to make the voter believe you truly stopped by. It leaves them with a good impression even though they didn't actually meet you.

Whenever I am campaigning I have two stacks of my campaign brochures with me, one to hand to people answering the door (that doesn't have the note), and the other with my pre-written "Sorry I Missed You" signed note. Depending on whether the door is answered or not, I just deal off the top, or bottom of the stack to leave the right brochure message. With this streamlining of the door-to-door process, my home visit volume went up considerably and a personalization effort was made even when no one was home. Leaving the personal message is almost as good as actually talking to someone because it shows them you personally stopped by. You receive the personal visit credit with out having to spend a lot of time writing out each note. Time is your enemy, because there are only a limited number of hours in a day that you can chase voters.

When To Go Door-to-Door?

Candidates will ring doorbells all hours of the day and night. Some will even do so on weeknights in the fall and spring when it gets dark at 5-6 pm. That is not a great way to make a first impression. It is probably closer to getting shot in the dark. First of all it's late enough that people get nervous when unknown strangers are ringing doorbells in the dark. Going door-to-door during the work week is not a real good idea because people have daily routines, eat meals at different times, give the kids baths and don't want to be pulled away from Monday Night Football or their favorite program to hear about your political aspirations. If you interrupt them you will not earn a good citizenship award, nor will they be very inclined to vote for you. Weeknight D-to-D is just a bad idea that should be avoided.

There are exceptions to the weeknight campaigning rule but it involves campaigning where the people come to you in the form of coffees, candidate debates, fundraisers and organized committee meetings.

Weekends are the best time to do the face-to-face campaigning because more people are home and most amenable to an interruption. Your hours for doorbell ringing should be no earlier than 10:30 am on weekend days and no later than 6:00 pm in the evening, earlier if it gets dark before that. You don't want to scare people, nor do you want to interrupt their weekend sleep-in, or get them up from the dinner table. You don't earn votes by getting people angry.

You should keep all of your weekends clear in the election timeline so that you can cover as much territory as possible. To keep momentum going during the workweek, you should schedule other get acquainted activities like coffees, fundraisers, speeches and such. These are events that people will come to if they have the time without you bothering them at home.

When you are out campaigning on the weekends, make an effort to spread yourself around the entire voting district so that if possible, people think you are

160

campaigning everywhere. Try to get a little word of mouth effort going where people are noting that you seem to be everywhere all over town. That creates a psychological problem for your opponents who will get reports that you have been here and there and tearing up the town with your campaign. There is another reason for working in all parts of town. You can look for additional sign locations, try to identify people who might offer to hold a coffee in a new neighborhood, and to generally strike fear in your opponents mind that you are everywhere.

So What's your Pitch?

When someone does answer the door, what should you say to him or her? That's a good question and one that you should work out in your head before you ring that first doorbell. Being tongue-tied is the last impression you want to leave with a voter.

This is where your issues review and your reasons for running come into play. Why are you running and what you stand for should be stated, but at the same time you can't expect to get too much into a few sentences. So you should offer a friendly introduction that can be expanded to your issues if the citizen has an interest in what you are saying. Say something like:

> **"Hello, Mr. Bohler, my name is Tom Renk**
> **I'm a candidate for Village Trustee. I wanted to introduce myself and hope that you will consider me when you vote April 1st. This campaign brochure outlines my beliefs and concerns for the Village."**

If you are the incumbent, then you should advise them that you are their current representative and that you hope they will re-elect you on election day. This quick introduction tells them what they need to know about you. Your name, the office you are seeking, and that you have personally visited with them. It also allows them to accept your brochure and say goodbye. In many cases that is exactly what will happen. You may have caught them busy making dinner, or with the Sunday football game on 3rd down with 3 to go. If you press your luck and try to engage them in conversation when they don't want to talk, they will resist and you may lose a vote rather than gain it.

You need to be able to read body language and understand human nature, so that in a few seconds, you can gauge how long a conversation should be and how quickly you release the ones that aren't interested. Sometimes a good indicator is the frown on their face or the fact that the door is about to hit your nose. Those are the easy ones to read. Over the years, I have had doors slammed in my face,

So What's your Pitch? 163

people have yelled at me to get off their property, they have threatened to turn the dog loose, and have said they don't vote. I have learned not to become offended because if you look down the block you will see hundreds of houses where people may be interested. Remind yourself that these people will some day need your help, when they have a zoning problem, or need a building permit for a fence, or have a neighbor who is playing loud music. Over the years, I have found what goes around comes around as well. And if it does you can be more gracious then these folks and help them out.

If you find that a resident does have some interest in what you say, you should definitely explore the interest and see what else you can discuss. About 5% will be pleased to see you and want to discuss an issue. These people are often one-issue folks, angry about something, and you may have just walked into the lion's den. But it is a way to discuss and learn about issues and you can let them know where you stand and that you care. The one-issue folks will not want to wander off of their personal issue but you can sometimes steer the conversation to the bigger picture and still satisfy their concern. These are people to ask for support with a sign or a donation.

When it is cold and miserable you will look forward to a chance to step out of the elements and warm up even if it means dueling with a voter. The really good folks will see that you are freezing and even offer you a cup of coffee, God bless them. The only problem with spending time indoors is that you are missing the opportunity to ring ten more doorbells that day because you have taken the homeowner up on the warmth and conversation. But look at the bright side, if you can really get the voter to like you and support you, the voter may talk to his neighbors and say you're the candidate they should all vote for. You get to warm up and win the election!

Talking about the cold and miserable weather, you should look at such weather as an opportunity to show the voters your determination. No matter how cold it is you should be out there ringing doorbells. Voters will think you're a little crazy, but also very committed. And that translates into sympathy and voter support. I remember a time when I was much younger and had a mustache while campaigning. It was so cold my breath was freezing on my mustache. But many people commented on my resolve and said they would vote for me if I were that committed. And lots of people were kind enough to invite me in to defrost the mustache.

In weather like that plan your door-to-door circuits so that you do about 40–50 homes up and down a block or two, ending up back at your car to warm up every hour or so. About an hour in the elements is about the right time before your face turns blue and you can't feel your extremities. The car heater and a hot cup of coffee will thaw you out while you update your polling lists with notes and comments. The weather actually becomes a campaign benefit because people remember a crazy candidate who visited them during a snowstorm.

When going door-to-door you should also keep in mind not to interrupt people when they are doing something important, like watching the Super Bowl game in late January. Super Bowl Sunday is one day that you shouldn't schedule ringing doorbells. It just aggravates people so concede the day. Rather, organize a fundraiser built around Super Bowl Sunday. All you need is someone with a large screen television, some beer, chips and dip, and you can charge people to come to the event. But remember to let them know ahead of time that it is a political fundraiser.

When walking the neighborhoods, and you see a bunch of cars at a house try to determine what kind of gathering it is. If it's a kid's birthday with balloons out front, skip the house, but if it is a neighborhood gathering and you wouldn't be imposing, ring the doorbell. I once received 27 signatures on my nomination papers at one house, saving me a lot of walking time. In another situation I was invited in and talked with numerous people because it was actually an organizational meeting for a school referendum, which I supported. These are situations where you have to play it by ear and consider your options. You may stumble into a windfall or a wasp's nest.

When you are going door-to-door be mindful of people's privacy, property, the laws, speed limits and even where you park your car when you start your walkabout. Residents are very protective of their properties, so shortening the distance between one house and the next by cutting across the lawn, or their favorite flowerbed, is a good way to lose the homeowners vote. Be respectful of lawns and flowers and always walk back to the sidewalk or street and then on to the next home. Someone is always watching either in the home just visited, or in the house across the street. Neighborhood Watch is very real and alive in most communities so pay attention to good manners and try not to alienate anyone.

If you are running in a community that is out in the far suburbs where the houses are on acre lots, spread way apart, you have your work cut out for you. In these cases shoe leather becomes a legitimate campaign expense category. While you may have to hoof through some of these wide-open spaces, there are other options for covering such neighborhoods including delivering brochure flyers with a team of supporters to spread the work out, or more costly postage mailings that are sent to the homes. But a personal visit even though it may be a long walk will still make the best impression. You have to determine whether you can afford the time to cover all the homes and then act accordingly.

What Can Happen, Will Happen!

Over the last 25 years of ringing doorbells and seeking votes, I have seen just about everything you could possibly imagine. I've seen homes that should be declared physically uninhabitable, children that should have been turned over to DCFS, dogs and animals that are out of control and even people who boldly answer the door naked as the day they were born. All of these situations could and probably will happen to you. You should be prepared to deal with them before you ring that first doorbell.

Dogs, big, little…. and mean!

The most prevalent problem is dogs that are protective of their domiciles. And you are nothing more than a trespasser when you come walking up to the house. Often the homeowners are oblivious to the fact they are harboring a dangerous animal that would just as soon eat your arm for breakfast. I 'm always wary when approaching a house, looking for signs of a dog. Dogs will often hear you and be hiding behind the door before you get to the door. If they bark and come bounding to the door I always heighten my awareness of the situation. If there is no screen door I get ready to slide my campaign brochure through the door when the homeowner opens it. Hopefully they will make an effort to keep the dog inside by only opening the door a bit. With a dog trying to eat me for lunch I make my pitch short, offer the brochure and start backing away.

If there is a screen door on the house, when you hear a dog barking, gently put your foot up against the screen door to prevent it from opening too wide so that Brutus can't get out. You will find that homeowners are often completely oblivious to their dogs preferred dining habits and will open the inner door as wide as possible without a care in the world, and Brutus will often try to make a break for you.

This gambit will save torn pants and dog bites. You quickly make your pitch while keeping your foot poised against the screen door, and then take off to end the frenzy. You may laugh, but I have been jumped a half dozen times over the years and I now use a pro-active defense to protect myself. I don't recommend any dog sprays or anything like that because you will only anger the voter whose little dog wanted you for lunch.

Small dogs tend to be even more dangerous because they can sneak through most door defenses and homeowners don't believe FiFi could hurt anyone. But they can if you let them, so plan ahead. Vigilance has prevented many dog bites.

Nudes at the Door!

"Politics gives guys so much power that they tend to behave badly around women. And I hope I never get into that."

—William J. Clinton

While this quote doesn't fit here perfectly, I just couldn't pass up the irony of our past President's words. Bill probably did some door-to-door campaigning in his early days and perhaps ran into this awkward situation. Having a nude person answer the door is a whole different experience than being attacked by a dog and simply holding the screen door with your foot to prevent injury. I wish I could accurately tell you how to deal with this phenomena but it is hard to explain, much less prepare for.

Nudes answering the door have confronted me on a number of occasions, with both male and female practitioners enjoying their personal freedoms to the limit. I guess there must be a lot of practicing nudists out there sitting around all day watching television or doing housework in their birthday suits. And these situations have never happened in the early morning when perhaps you got someone out of bed. It is always late afternoon when most normal people have bothered to put on something for the day.

The other truism is that in my personal experience, these folks have never graced the pages of Playboy, or even the beefcake calendars. These exhibitionists are never movie stars or swimsuit models. They are just very ordinary people with all the usual, unattractive appendages. So what do you do when all this epidermis decides to answer the door?

My suggestion is strong eye contact. You try to keep your eyes above the Mason Dixon line and concentrate on delivering your usual pitch, offer them a brochure and get ready to move on. Often they answer the door in their birthday suit just to get a reaction. So you must try not to react, but that will probably be a reaction in itself! I had one young woman offer me to come in out of the cold

168

for a cup of coffee, but I politely declined and offered my brochure like the pro that I was. I was out of there as fast as I could walk on snow-covered sidewalks. I'm sure she got a good laugh and I hope she had clothes on when she voted for me!

One of the exposures you will have from all of this door-to-door campaigning is that you will see all sorts of crazy things through the door and unbelievable house cleaning issues when you are occasionally invited in. You will be shocked at how people live but try hard not to react in any way because it will invariably offend them. Remember you are trying to earn votes, not be the house and garden fashion police handing out citations for bad housekeeping.

Children

Neighborhood kids will often be out and about on weekends playing in the yards and riding their bikes. They are usually quite inquisitive and will hang around and follow you as you go door-to-door. Sometimes they will say their parents are not home, which always surprises me, or that Mom is in the bathtub, which surprises me even more. So I adjust my effort by just leaving a brochure, or by asking them to give it to Mom. Who knows, maybe the brochure will share the bath and you might get a thorough reading of the document. Don't carry on any long conversations with kids because the snoopy lady two houses down the block is always watching and she will call the police in a heartbeat if she thinks the Boston Strangler is roaming around on her block.

Another thing you will find surprising is how many parents are so casual (lazy may be the better word) about allowing their young 3 and 4 year-old kids to open the door on their own, without making any effort to find out who is knocking. The kids often come to the door without clothes on at 4 pm in the afternoon. It makes you wonder. In a situation like that you should ask if mom or dad is there. Hopefully that will produce a real voter. What really scares me is when young children answer the door and readily volunteer that their parents are not home, or readily invite you into the house and a parent is nowhere in sight. In situations like this you should decline the invitation, give them a brochure and quickly excuse myself.

The Elderly

Our older citizens are usually pretty friendly to candidates. That can be true for a variety of reasons, but I have always found that to be the case. They may have a personal agenda in mind or they may just like the fact that there is someone at the door to talk to. Over the years I have had elderly people ask me to do favors for them like getting the Sunday newspaper at the end of the drive, or putting in a light bulb because they can't reach. I did these things because I genuinely felt they could use the help. I have drawn the line at cutting lawns and doing windows.

The elderly will often invite you in because they don't get to see as many people and look forward to carrying on a real conversation. While you may be initially reluctant to get involved in lengthy conversations, you may find that these senior citizens usually have a wealth of knowledge about their community history, their neighborhoods, all the crazy people up and down the street, and seem to have a very good grasp of the issues.

You will find them to be articulate, somewhat opinionated, but very willing to talk about issues in depth. Getting into a good conversation about current events can sharpen your ability to discuss them when you have to be in front of an audience or when the press comes calling.

You should welcome a chance to sit down with an elderly resident because you can always learn something. A cup of hot coffee and a few minutes of warmth away from the elements can be a treat. When someone invites you in, go ahead, but keep your wits about you. They may be really checking you out and they have an extensive network in the community, so you want to make a good impression.

Some elected officials will tell you spending this much time with any age voter is a waste of your very limited time. But it is just the opposite, because you learn all sorts of things about your community and the people within it. The same is true if you can find out where all the retired folks meet each morning for coffee. If you can find that gathering spot at your local McDonalds or the neighborhood restaurant, ask if you can join them, introduce yourself and then listen to what they have to say. You may not like all their comments but you will learn a lot.

In my home community the farmers are still a major part of the local culture and a good sized group of them can always be found every morning at the local gas stations having coffee and good conversation. But you have to get up early to catch these farmers. They like to assemble early from 6:30–7:30 in the morning and they are long gone by 8:00 am back to their chores.

If you want to know what is going on in a farm community, just find that group and see if you can join them some mornings. You will get an earful, but it will tell you more than you would ever find out in any other part of town. The toughest part may be in getting them to allow you to sit in. If you know one of the regulars ask him if he would take you along and introduce you to the group. Then if you get to sit down at the table, don't be too quick to jump in and say your piece. Let them get to know you and feel you out a bit. They will know why you are there and just being there will tell them a lot about you. Get a group like this supporting you and you will have a strong back-channel network that will let all sorts of people in on your election quest. But also keep in mind that it could go the other way and they find they have little in common with you.

Door-to-Door De-Briefing

After a long day of trudging around town, it is important to come home and de-brief yourself before you forget what you learned from the voters, where new sign locations can be located, and what issues you were not aware of. This is something you should do every time you return home, because if you wait to write these things down, you will forget half of them. (Again, experience is speaking).

You should update the coverage on your large map of the district. Seeing your map being slowly colored in after covering sections of town can be very therapeutic. It will give you encouragement to keep going. It's almost as good a feeling as that hot shower will be. Because of the limited number of weekends available for campaigning, crossing out the covered areas eventually shows you are covering the entire district. And your morale benefits.

When in the field, carry your polling lists for the specific neighborhoods your in. Make small notes right on the lists after visiting people, noting their concerns, and what you may need to get for them. Following this approach will make a messy field list, but that is why you have a clean one at home where you can transfer all the notes. Each note should be reviewed to capture whatever needs to be accomplished. More importantly, the notes should be converted to various to-do lists and if follow-up is required, acted on quickly.

You should regularly share your findings with your campaign committee for their insights. If you identify a new issue that hasn't surfaced yet, it may give you an edge at the next debate or town meeting. Do your homework and make sure the issue is real and you truly understand its component parts. If further investigation is needed, either get on it yourself, or have a committee member run it down. Visit City Hall to obtain additional insights and background, and if need be, report back to the citizen that raised the issue. You will earn their vote for your diligence.

I have found that de-briefing yourself is the best way to stay on top of things, even when your first inclination is to take that hot shower or take a nap. Spend the 15 minutes necessary to unload all the data you have collected so that you will retain it before you collapse. If you wait until the next day, you will miss most of it. Then go take that shower and get off your feet.

Publicity

"Today's public figures can no longer write their own speeches or books, and there is some evidence that they can't read them either."
—Gore Vidal

Once you have determined that your candidacy is a go, that is the day you should start thinking about all the publicity you will need, to gain visibility in the community and momentum to win the election. Publicity can take many forms, from simply being exposed to segments of the population, to formal press releases that chronicle the efforts of your candidacy, and to media exposure that you seek or arrange. In each campaign there are multiple opportunities to gain publicity and exposure. But you must seek them out and exploit them to benefit.

There are all sorts of events and appearances you can attend, and often they can assist in gaining exposure and they won't cost a dime. Have your committee map out a list of community events that will take place during the campaign. Things like festivals, dinners, church events, club meetings, children's sports nights, school programs, and like events. Check out whether the organizing committee's will allow you to set up some sort of booth or desk. Perhaps you would be allowed to hand out brochures, balloons, or some trinket that has your name on it. In many cases if you let the organizers know you are there they may gladly note your attendance, and may even allow you to distribute your brochure, or say something to the crowd. It doesn't hurt to ask. All they can say is no. It's a good way to be seen in the community and get the visibility going.

In Chicago, there are all sorts of parades for all sorts of ethnic groups, and you can bet that every politician within miles will try to walk the parade route showing their interest and support, so that they can garner that group support at election time. Often they will walk or ride in the parade and their supporters will hand out literature along the streets. The St. Patrick's Day parade in Chicago brings out national candidates each year and they all try to jockey for a spot walking with Mayor Daley, to be cast in his Irish spell of good candidate fortune.

You should also become familiar with local communication options to reach out to the public. This could include newspapers, local radio and television stations, neighborhood association newsletters, church bulletins and coupon fliers. Determine what the circulation numbers of each is and how they interface with your demographics.

A citywide newspaper may have poor coverage in your particular district, thus you would be wasting time and effort, especially if you are paying for expensive advertising. The newspaper should have demographic reports of their readership, segmented by zip code that they will share with you. Review these figures before making expensive advertising purchases. You may find that the local free paper gives better bang for your buck.

A radio station may have a wide coverage area but may also be the station with all the specific community information coverage you need. If the station is the one your town turns to for school closings and violent weather bulletins, it may be the one that you would consider having your local election press releases sent to.

If you are in a smaller community the local newspaper may only come out once or twice a week. You should buy a copy, or order a subscription so that you could analyze the kind of news coverage it offers on local government affairs. You may find that the newspaper is starving for news and good copy and will readily print your story if they know about you. This is a perfect situation for your candidacy and could be very helpful in getting you elected.

Once you have assessed the various communication options you may have available to you, should spend then spend some time figuring out what all the issues are, or will be. With the assistance of your Kitchen Cabinet you should draft short statements on your positions because once you approach these communication outlets they will ask you what you think about all the issues of the day. So be prepared before you seek them out.

"Elect Courtney's Daddy"

Each contact you develop through your community, work, neighborhood and school ties can become a valuable asset. As a case in point, I would like to tell you a story about one of my early campaigns and how my daughter helped me get elected.

Many years ago, my eldest daughter was in first grade and my wife and I were very involved in school and community activities. One day, Courtney was silently watching me prepare my aldermanic campaign signs in the basement. I was engrossed in cutting stakes, stapling and mounting hundreds of signs for the following weeks distribution. Unbeknownst to me she decided she wanted to help me out. She and her playmates all decided to make election signs of their own. They got out their crayons and colored paper and started making signs that said:

"Elect Courtney's Daddy"

The signs were hand drawn, used a variety of colors and looked beautiful in their simplicity. These four kids took them home and put them in their bedroom windows. Before long I noticed that a number of these little colorful signs were turning up in living room windows as well. Before I knew it a number of other first graders had climbed on the bandwagon and had signs at their houses too, showing their support for Courtney's dad. Mind you, not my name, not even my last name, just Courtney. While the kids didn't really know what they were doing, their childlike effort had a very profound effect in the neighborhood and with many of the parents. When I rang a doorbell, the parents wanted to meet Courtney's Dad. All of a sudden, I had some sorely needed visibility.

Then additional people, including other parents started commenting on the signs when I saw them at school, coffee's, or at the bank. Many people wanted to meet and see who Courtney's Daddy was because my name wasn't even on the signs. I still believe I received a considerable number of votes from "Elect Courtney's Daddy" signs and my little non-voting helpers. If I had been smarter back then, I would have had someone call the press to do a human interest story on these creative signs and I would have gotten a photo article and even more mileage out of it. It was a great shot in the arm and I'm pleased to report I won because of Courtney, unseating an incumbent. Courtney still supports all my campaign efforts and now she can vote!

I originally conceived that this book would be called "Elect Courtney's Daddy" but realized that it would be somewhat difficult to market and have candidates recognize this as an election how-to-book.

Newspapers

You should initially put together a campaign announcement about your candidacy and put in as much background as you can, outlining the reasons for running for office, your interests and positions on issues, your background and experience. Then personally visit the newspaper office, and try to get an interview with the Editor. Introduce yourself and see if you can get a conversation going. With a little luck, the Editor will take your Press Announcement and print a story in the next edition. With a little luck he or she may print everything that you submit. Hence the reason you would write a lengthy piece covering all the campaign bases.

While visiting the local newspaper you should also have one of those photographs we talked about earlier to run with the announcement. If the Editor prints the whole announcement as you have written it, you then will have a great resource for getting future information out to the public. That photo then goes into the file they will create on you and it may get used again in future campaign articles. Make the photo one that you can live with, not one that has your hair blowing sideways. You want to earn votes not scare people off.

You may find that small town newspapers are very willing to print any copy because they are usually desperate for the column inches to support the paper. That can work to your advantage. The secret is to give them what they want. To do that, just write the press announcement as if you are answering basic questions they would ask if they were interviewing you: who, what, where and when. Follow this approach and you will have a great publicity campaign started.

Once you know that they will appreciate the copy you offer, start sending press announcements and position papers on a regular basis. Every time you are involved in something important enough to let the people know what is going on, prepare a release. Some get printed and some don't but keep them coming. Some of the activities or events that could typically be covered by a press release (and their title) include:

- For filing Nomination Papers **"Renk Files For Board"**
- Various Speeches to groups **"Renk speaks to PTA"**
- Endorsements **"Teachers Endorse Renk"**
- Positions on Issues **"Renk supports Road-Widening"**
- Updates on Campaign **"Renk visits half of Village**
- Committee Additions **"Judge Johnson Joins Renk Team"**
- Yard Signs **"Renk distributes 300 signs to residents"**
- Campaign Updates **"Renk visits Senior Citizen Home"**
- D-to-D Brochure Drop **"50 Workers take Renk to Voters"**
- Election Day Voting Plans **"Renk offers Van service to Polls"**

There is no limit to the number of releases that can be issued, only to the number of stories that the local press might actually pick up and run. Again you won't know what amount of coverage might get picked up until you try. Come up with various headlines and stories if for no other reason than to rattle your opponents. Always make sure they see them even if the press doesn't pick them up. That way you can keep your opponents off balance.

Give editors and publishers good phone number contacts where you can be reached, or give them your campaign chair's contact information so you can be called for comment on an issue. If a story is about to be printed that concerns you, the newspaper should know how to contact you for comment. Also, you may get a lead on a less than flattering story that may be coming out and it will give you time to initiate damage control or put a different spin on the issue. Staying in touch just makes good sense.

If you are not a writer who can prepare such releases, find someone on your Campaign Committee who can and have that person cultivate the personal relationship with the Editor. Touch base with the Editor regularly during a campaign. Usually they will cry uncle if the volume is too much and then you can develop another source of communication, perhaps at the radio station.

Radio

With a radio station the same approach can work although you would be approaching the station manager or a reporter offering them sound bites that could be used on the air. In a situation like this, issue the same press release and offer to be available for an interview, or for some pre-recorded sound bites. If you make yourself accessible they will often call you for insights on an issue they are working on. Working with the press has its advantages and disadvantages but overall, if you are careful and mindful of everything you say, it can be advantageous to the campaign. Such coverage will also drive your opponents crazy if they have not figured out how to do it.

While you can completely control what you write in a press release, it is a much more difficult equation to control what you say when someone is asking for a live quote for the newspaper or the media. For these situations you need to think ahead about what you will say in response to questions. If you have ever watched people being interviewed on the talk shows or news programs, you will see people totally unprepared in a complete meltdown, and others who have complete control of the situation.

It is important that you carefully think about what you are about to say before you actually say it. Remember that as a candidate for office, you are in the public eye, and once you say something it will be attributed to you, whether it is right or wrong, good or bad, probably forever. Once it is out of your mouth you have to live with the statement. That being said there are ways to control these situations.

I remember watching Senator Hillary Clinton discuss her recent book about life in the Clinton White House, and when she didn't want to directly answer a thorny question, you could see that she had a prepared comment or catch phrase that diffused the question and changed the subject. Her response would fill airtime but wouldn't really answer the probing question. Often it was a funny response or turned the question into a harmless thought. But she was totally prepared to diffuse these questions.

Being prepared is the most important thing you can do to effectively use publicity to your advantage. Think through your issues and positions, prepare your responses and try not to venture off the planned path in responding to questions. Use phrases you are comfortable with. President George W. Bush is not the best public speaker and he often uses tried and true catch phrases to sidestep questions and to steer clear of difficult subjects. If a question takes you into uncharted waters, try to steer the question back to familiar territory. If that cannot be done, then simply state you don't have a position on that matter, or have 'no comment' at this time.

One way to get comfortable with the material you may need to talk about is to set up a friendly practice session with your Kitchen Cabinet. Have them ask you some questions and you can practice your responses. The President of the United States does this to prepare for debates with challengers. They actually call it Debate Camp with some senior aide filling in for the opponent. This stand-in challenger is just as well prepped and actually tries to throw curve ball comments at the President to see how he reacts, before such things really happen live before a national audience. Even the professional politicians use these methods to prepare so why not you.

Try to have someone ask you questions ahead of time to try out your responses and get more comfortable with the material. Have your spouse or a Committee member prep you for various interviews and you will do fine when the time comes to offer a comment on the record or a sound bite for the media. This is even more important if you will actually be on the small screen in front of people. By the way, when you are having campaign events always invite the press, because they may actually show up and cover the event. But be prepared because they may also want to ask questions of you or the people attending. By being prepared with answers to questions you can channel the press attendance into positive exposure.

Television

If your community is larger and there is television or cable coverage in the area, you will need to work harder to get any airtime through this medium but it too can offer great visibility. You should still be fully prepared to answer reporter questions so that if the opportunity does present itself you can make it work for you.

You can also create a little bit of news yourself. The secret here is to become actively involved in the community where larger events and activities may catch the attention of the TV station. A good example would be to join a demonstration (that you can support) asking for better police protection in a neighborhood, or to tear down a blighted building, or raise money for a new park. The organizers of such a demonstration once they know you are supportive may want to have you address the crowd and that could give you much needed exposure. If it gets media coverage you are front and center supporting the cause.

Another example could be your interest in the de-forestation of parkland. You could pre-announce you are taking a stand on this issue and show up threatening to throw yourself in front of the bulldozers, just in time for the 6:00 pm news. If your committee has done their homework to alert the press of your participation at the demonstration, you may obtain some exposure and possible voter support. The park group will also appreciate your effort to bring greater exposure to their cause. Just get out of the way of the bulldozers before they grind you up!

Another thing to look at is the cost of buying time on the local cable station or even commercial time on all the cable channels that have popped up in recent years. The costs of advertising on cable stations can be quite inexpensive depending on time of day and station. Get a hold of the rate cards because you may be surprised at how inexpensive it actually is. Or you may want to inquire about buying a half or full hour of cable time and produce your own infomercial. If you could afford to buy the time, you could set up a point—counterpoint type interview program to discuss issues and define your positions on community subjects.

If you buy the time you can control how the program is delivered. You could hire an interviewer, or utilize someone from your Campaign Committee to ask questions of you.

You should also check out other opportunities to gain exposure like buying small ads in the church newspapers, the free tabloids that are distributed in convenience stores, and even advertising opportunities in the local theatre that run before the films being shown. Look for opportunities that will work in your community.

Speaking Opportunities

There are numerous opportunities in any election cycle to gain press exposure. You can look for speaking opportunities, and you should offer to participate in discussion groups, organize neighborhood meetings and speak up at council meetings to make yourself seen. Have your Campaign Committee start identifying opportunities and see if there is some way to get yourself involved. Often all it takes is a call to the event or program organizer asking them if you could participate as a candidate. You may find they would willingly give you a platform to speak and if the press is already planning to cover the event you have a bonus situation. Just ask Jesse Jackson the civil rights activist. He is known for showing up for all sorts of political demonstrations, controversial press briefings, and national and local problems that give him publicity and exposure. And he usually gets a sound bite on the local and national news. If anything he is over-exposed, but he seems to think it is a positive thing to be everywhere.

If you make an effort to explore publicity opportunities and your opponents do not, you will have an edge over them because the public will be more likely to know your candidacy. And that means you may earn their vote. As you develop these publicity opportunities don't share them with your opponents, let them figure it all out on their own. Why give them access to the opportunities you created for yourself.

At various civic meetings and programs, try to determine ways to intelligently insert yourself into the discussion. Don't just jump in to hear yourself talk, but instead wait for the right time to say something appropriate to define your position or issue. Make your comments count. If the issue is of concern to the community the press may already be there, so don't be surprised if they come over to you for further comment. As a candidate you are the more public figure and what you say will be perceived as more important. Thus you need to think about what you would say ahead of time. All that position writing and practice in answering questions will come in handy in this situation.

Welcome such questioning because it may give you another exposure in the newspaper or on the radio, and you only have three months to make an impression with the public. The secret is to carefully think about what you will say and then say it......and nothing more. If the press has follow up questions that deviates from your prepared remarks, politely repeat yourself and re-state what you have already said. That way you better control the situation. After you have handled a few of these inquiries you will get a feeling for it and it will become second nature. That's how all of those congressmen and Senators deal with the press. They plan ahead and have their comments almost memorized. That way they rarely look foolish and have more control over the situation.

Public Forums/Candidate Nights

In most community elections some group or civic organization will sponsor a Candidates Night, where all the candidates are invited to speak about their concerns and the issues before the voters. Many first time candidates will dread such an event because they are uncomfortable getting in front of a crowd and they are reluctant to expose themselves to such scrutiny. But this is a great opportunity to distinguish yourself from the others and pull ahead of the pack of candidates if you handle the situation well.

First of all you have very little to be frightened about. My experience has shown that most of the people in attendance at these events are family and committee members who already know you. So you really have very little to prove to them. This is true for all the other candidates as well. In fact if you eliminate the supporters, family, and committee members there may only be a few real voters in the room.

So relax, you won't win or lose many votes. As soon as you accept that fact, you quickly realize that you have very little to worry about. One exception is when multiple candidates are running for multiple seats on the ballot, which means a voter can vote for three or four candidates. In this situation you may have a great opportunity to pick up votes from the other candidate's supporters, if you can impress them with your delivery.

The secret is to concentrate on using the event to good advantage because the press will usually be in attendance reporting so all the people who didn't attend may gain some insight. That is the real audience you should be speaking to, because they are covering the event for the public in general. This is a perfect opportunity to set the record straight on what your issues and positions are. It is also an opportunity to differentiate yourself from your opponents and take the high ground on issues.

You should do some homework prior to such an event. Clearly understand what the forum format, schedule and agenda is going to be, whether candidate statements will be allowed, whether prepared issue questions are to be asked, what those questions might be, and whether the public will be able to ask questions from the floor. All of these options will dictate how to prepare for the event.

If prepared statements are allowed, ask how many minutes you will be given because you want to pack as much punch as possible into the time frame. The basis of your statement might reference your campaign brochure, which you should readily have available, but might also raise a new issue that has come up since the brochure was first printed.

In a situation like this, you also want to determine the order of presentation by the candidates, and if possible volunteer to go first. The reason you want to go first is to set the pace for all the other candidates. You want to be the leader on an issue rather than the one following. Many candidates will not be terribly excited about participating at all because they hate to get up in front of a group. This is where you can excel by beating back your personal demons and standing tall. You need to show the voters that you are capable, and are the person for the job.

Always volunteer to go first so that you can set the pace, identify and define the issues, and be the first one to speak about them. That leaves all the other candidates with "me too" comments, rehashing what you have already said. All the other candidates have to try to measure up to you. To do this you have to put away your fears of standing in front of a crowd. You will find that once you get started you forget about your fears and can use the first position to great advantage.

If you can't be the first speaker to respond to a question, then use the extra waiting time to formulate a stronger comment that will still differentiate your opinions from the first speaker. Rather than giving a "me too" response, try to distinguish yourself by raising a new point, or taking an entirely different approach to the question. Make your answer interesting and the voters will remember your comments better.

When the event is almost over try to get in the last comments on the program to leave all the voters with a good last impression. One suggestion is to simply thank everyone for attending, especially if the organizers are not doing that from the podium. If you use the forum opportunity correctly you can use it to build your visibility in the community.

If prepared questions are part of the program format, try to find out what those questions will be ahead of time. Sometimes they are pre-determined and even pre-announced, and then you can really prepare dynamic responses for them. But often the questions are kept secret to give everyone an equal chance to think on their feet. In this case going first may not be the best approach as you only have a few minutes to formulate a response. In a situation like this, guess at the questions and develop a number of potential responses. You can practice delivering them with your committee. You may already have such prepared summaries from creating your briefing book. Find out if you could bring your briefing book with you to the podium. If you can take it with you, just refer to answer you already developed. You will look strong and gain the public's confidence.

The secret is to pre-determine solid responses to potential questions, to set yourself apart from your competition. You are trying to stake out clearly defined positions. Otto von Bismarck was credited with saying, "Politics is the art of the possible." You want to make people believe in you, take positions that distinguish you from the others, and stand for what you believe in.

If the Forum encourages questions from the general public, this is a situation that your friends and committee members should actively participate in. Try to prep them to ask certain questions that will distinguish you from the others and will allow you to gain even greater exposure. Don't be afraid to use this approach because the other candidate's friends will be doing the same for them. You probably shouldn't ask your spouse to ask the questions, but someone that has your best interest in mind can raise their hand and ask a question for you and the others. They can and should ask pointed questions that you want to answer, or questions that will define your reasons for running for office, or that set you apart from the other candidates.

If you know a tough question will be asked and you have a strong response prepared, you will stand out in the crowd. In this situation, perhaps your questioner should ask your opponent first, to allow your response to be even stronger. You want to use the format to your advantage, thus you should give it careful thought and set a plan.

At these kind of forums you should always plan on arriving early to get the lay of the land. Park your car with signs in the windows near the door so that everyone arriving will walk past it. Bring extra yard signs and stack them in a corner of the hall in case anyone asks for one. Bring campaign brochures and see if you can put them out on the chairs, or have someone hand them out to the audience. As people wait for the event to start, they may read the whole thing. You may find people who express an interest in supporting your candidacy. Distinguish yourself during the presentation and voters will offer to help, put up a sign or offer to hold a coffee. After a program hang around to talk with voters and ask if you were effective.

Encourage your family and committee members to critically critique your performance so that you can learn from the experience. Invariably they will also critique the other candidates and that information may allow you to exploit some weakness that you may not have noticed at a future event. As an example, if another candidate got extremely defensive, what triggered his reaction? Did it make him look less like a viable candidate? That could be explored at future meeting. If another candidate did extremely poorly in the public forum situation, encourage the organizing body to hold another program in other parts of town. You have to exploit all the opportunities if you are going to win the election in the three short months you have to make a good impression.

Think of these political forums as very necessary public exposure opportunities and approach them with forethought and a plan of action and you will earn votes, gain exposure and intimidate your opponents.

Other Public Exposure

There will be many chances for you to gain public exposure and visibility in the election cycle. You just need to figure out where they are by carefully looking for opportunities. If you are involved in school affairs there will invariably be a school event or PTA meeting that would allow you some exposure. While you can't just jump up on a soapbox and start ranting about issues, you should talk to the organizers and let them know you are running for office. They may introduce you and other candidates all at the same time. If some of the other candidates are not there you will have gained a minor advantage. The organizers might even be willing to give you more exposure, and you should have a short introduction speech prepared t o get some visibility. After being introduced or saying something, always take advantage by sticking around and working the room to see if you can identify voters and supporters.

No matter where you are in the community, always keep looking for chances to spread the word, introduce yourself, or find a way to gain some visibility. My wife says that I'm always on stage. That too is something to keep in mind. Being a candidate is kind of like being on stage, subject to scrutiny at all times. It's like living in a fishbowl where everyone can see you.

You don't want to be seen doing something illegal, drinking to excess, speeding through the neighborhoods, or sleeping in church to name a few that quickly come to mind. You don't want to be caught on camera walking into an off-track betting parlor, because the press may run that clip over and over again just prior to the election. It doesn't look good and will create doubt that you are the person that should be elected.

Another good example is how people might see you at the local Mall on a Saturday yelling at your kids to keep up or spanking them when they throw a tantrum. Your candidacy creates an invisible stage that moves with you wherever you go while you are a candidate. What you do want to be seen doing is positive things like pitching in on a neighborhood project, teaching Sunday School, umpiring the Little League Game, and volunteering in your community. Keep in mind that image of politicians kissing babies to earn votes. It's a warm fuzzy, but it makes the candidate look good.

Always presume that someone is watching your every move. That could include how you handle yourself in the grocery parking lot fighting over a spot with an unknown citizen, who turns out to be a voter. After he recognizes you he may not vote for you, but you have to also figure he will tell every one of his neighbors and the folks at church on Sunday that you are a jerk. Presume you are on stage all the time during a political race and act accordingly. If you are perceived as an asset to the community you have a better chance of representing that community.

Looking for Votes

While you are searching for events to gain visibility also look for hidden votes that you might not have otherwise noticed. These include voters in senior citizen homes and retirement communities, voters with a special axe to grind because of some impending problem or battle, or young people who may only be coming of voting age in the months preceding an election.

Senior citizens always seem to be registered voters as they take their democratic privileges seriously, and you would be surprised at how well versed they can be on community issues. This may be because they have more time to read and discuss these issues over coffee at McDonalds every morning. Have you ever noticed that the same group of retirees shows up at the local McDonalds or restaurant? Introducing yourself as a local candidate may be a good way to gain some insights into the campaign and hear some thoughts on the issues. If you approach them and are willing to listen they will give you an ear full and will listen to you as well.

If your political district has a senior citizens home try to seek out the administrator and ask for permission to do a little prospecting for votes. Who knows, maybe they will even create an in-house public forum for you. Either way, ask if any of these senior citizens would like to vote on Election Day and offer to get them rides to the polling place.

As a young man, I saw my Dad lose an Aldermanic race in this manner. His incumbent opponent was on the Board of Directors of a Retirement Home and had great access to all the folks living at the home. My father thought this opponent would have tied up all the votes. After the election he realized that one of the other Board members was a friend of his and could have had great influence in lining up votes had he known to ask.

My father's opponent even rented a bus on Election Day and took over one hundred people to the polls. The senior citizens loved the trip and willingly voted for the man who made it possible. My Dad lost by about 100 votes! While this is an expensive way to gather votes it works if you need a bunch more to put you over the top. More often than not you can find a couple of campaign committee members who will volunteer to shuttle seniors to and from the election site. If you can find votes that way offer to personally drive them if you have to!

Identifying voters who are angry about an issue or some community problem can also be a good way to generate votes, that is, if you can readily stand on their side of the issue, and can get them to believe you might help them resolve the problem. This can be a dicey challenge because you haven't yet been elected, and are powerless to prevent their concern from happening. But you may be able to show them you will support their efforts as best you can by offering a different perspective than the incumbents are offering.

As an example, over the years I have come to cherish the many historical components of the communities I have lived in. In one election the Historical Society was fighting the Village Board to save an old building and to designate an area as a historical area. I found that I could readily support their values and when I made that known to the Society I gained almost complete support from their members for my candidacy.

Always try to determine what the real issues are and invariably you will find special groups that have taken a position on these issues. It may be that they are against power lines being put in their area, or that they want to see the Library expanded, or a new children's park developed. With every issue there are folks who will have an opinion one way or another. You need to determine what the issues are and identify the people who care about them. These individuals will be the voters interested in what you have to say.

A good example would be a street-widening project that will cause a good number of mature trees to be torn down in the rebuilding process. The citizens are desperately trying to save the trees, and upset about being saddled with the cost of improvements. Its one of those situations that can't be won or lost by you, but you can advise them you will have their interests in mind when elected. They may be so fed up with the existing elected officials that as a new candidate you may earn their vote. But in this situation, it is a double-edged sword because eventually those road improvements will need to be done. Most communities have five and ten year road improvement programs in place that evaluate road repair and replacement options. Because replacement costs are so high, the community doesn't frivolously schedule such road improvements. It is usually truly needed work. In situations like this I try to understand the concerns of the citizens and keep their viewpoints in mind when elected.

There are all sorts of controversial issues in a campaign and you should try to identify the issues and the people that are affected by them. Always remember that for every person against an issue there is probably also someone in favor of it. You have to figure out what your position and ethics will be on the issue and then align yourself with one group or the other. Do your positioning carefully, and discuss the issue with your advisors and campaign committee. Use your campaign committee to help you evaluate which side of an issue you should be on and then stick to that position even though it may be unpopular with a certain segment of voters.

The public will not tolerate a politician who wavers on issues and can't take a strong position. That is why politicians say the buck stops on their desk. You have to make the decisions and then stand by them. If you can't find any issues to build campaign support, you may need to find something that you can rally the troops around. That is where all that initial research and background work comes in. Talk to people, read the local newspaper and ask what's on people's minds.

In a recent campaign I was the only candidate that was concerned about the continued growth of a small regional airport, owned by another neighboring community located right in the middle of our community. It was created way out in the farm fields when first built. Our Village had grown around it completely and yet we had no say about its growth and expansion. At public forums, I started raising the issues of growth pointing out that as an expanding regional airport with a mile long runway, it could eventually support commercial traffic that would bring all sorts of additional planes and traffic into the quiet community we currently had. Once the subject was raised a good number of citizens began to think about the consequences of such growth to their neighborhoods, their properties and land values. I made it a campaign issue and I had a drivers seat vantage point because I had looked at the big picture implications of this growth. The issue is a now a very real one and the village has taken a strong position concerning this growth without being involved in the process. I identified an issue that none of the other candidates had taken positions on. It gave me visibility and creditability in the minds of the voters.

It is important that you look for all the community issues, both visible and not so visible, and then evaluate how you feel about them. As an elected official you may have to take a position, so you might as well see what is out there while you are a candidate and use it to your advantage to gain public awareness for your candidacy.

Election Pacing

You will usually find there is general ambivalence to the election in the early weeks of the campaign. That is to be expected, as the general public does not have the same zeal that you have for the campaign trail. You may remember that I suggested building an Election Timeline covering all the weeks between your initial announcement to run and the election itself. This will be an invaluable tool to assist you in ramping your efforts up as the campaign progresses. You want to pick up the intensity of activity each week as Election Day approaches. Then the public will begin to notice that you are a candidate.

You can spend the early weeks of the campaign quietly going door-to-door, passing Nomination papers and talking to people on an individual basis. This is a time when things are less frenzied and you can take the time to discuss issues and talk at length to constituents. This is also when you should have fund-raisers and coffees to line up money and help that you will need for the latter part of the election effort.

Then about four to six weeks out you should make an effort to become even more visible all around the community, making appearances at the school functions, at socials, at public forums and at the public council meetings. It is important to be seen all over the community, involved in programs, attending events, volunteering your time to help the community, and letting people see that you are already involved.

Use of yard signs are one of the major pacing components leading up to the final push. Wait until about two weeks before the election to put out all your yard signs. You could have the signs out much earlier, but you get just as much bang for your buck on a tighter time frame. When signs are put out too early, people tend to ignore them and you will lose a lot of them to weather and other damage. Waiting until just before the election and the voters get a large imposing display of your candidacy, a visual reminder that you are in the race. The election becomes more focused in their minds.

Then in that last full weekend before the election, you should try to have a major literature drop, or a mailing to the voters, to get that last impression before they vote. A strong finish is essential to registering your name in the minds of the voter.

If you have the luxury of a lot of help you might also organize a phone tree call around, although this could become a negative. With all the recent abuses of telemarketing calls angering people, you don't want to get the voters upset at the last minute because they will blame you and carry that frustration into the voting booth.

Timing is everything so you need to look for opportunities to make visual impressions on the voters. It may be as simple as parking a car with a car top carrier at the Little League Field each Saturday and at your church each Sunday Morning. By the way make sure you park it legally and in the appropriate spaces, don't park in the handicap spot if you don't have the sticker allowing you to do so. It can be as simple as standing outside the bakery on the weekends and saying hello to folks, or standing outside the commuter train station from 6:00–8:30 am handing out literature. People tend to read your brochure while sitting on the train for a half hour.

The bottom line is you need to manufacture opportunities to make yourself visible to the public and the community as a whole. Running for public office is time consuming, tedious and frustrating, but remember that you chose to run and now you need to do everything possible to win.

Technology Campaigning

In recent years, campaigning has taken on a whole new look with the advent of computers, websites and e-mail. Computers have made the job of identifying voters, categorizing them and targeting them much easier to coordinate, freeing you to spend more quality time interacting with the voters. In the past you would spend weeks pouring over the manual voting lists and trying to glean good voter information from meager records. The computer and information age has changed all that.

Computers can be effectively used to create all sorts of campaign materials, with user-friendly software, allowing people with minimal design training to create great little brochures and campaign literature. These brochures can also be quickly re-designed and re-printed in mid campaign to emphasize a particular issue or change the focus of the campaign. Your opponent can also use this same design creativity and speed, so be flexible to challenges and changes that may come at you throughout the campaign.

The ease of creating and using Websites has also changed campaigning. You can now create your own campaign website and try to drive people to the site to elevate issues, lay out your vision, examine your positions, offer to help, and to make a donation. It can give you strong visibility if you make the site attractive and interactive and it is easy to navigate. As more people are adding computers and e-mail it becomes a great way to get into the homes and minds of the voters.

If you haven't yet given thought to a website you should do so. With a little funding you can create a great site that will serve you well. Find someone that understands and develops websites and see if they will be on your committee. It will probably be one of your kids friends but they can help just as well as someone else. E-mail may be the next best way to access voters. While polling lists do not offer e-mail addresses yet, I am guessing that this communication method will become a factor in the future. For now you can try to identify the e-mail addresses of voters by building a database and gathering e-mail addresses wherever possible. You may find e-mail addresses in church directories, school lists, and neighborhood association lists.

You can check to see if such lists are available for purchase. If they are, buy one before they are taken off the market, as this information will allow you to make campaign pitches for almost nothing. Once you develop such a database, you need to be careful with it and not abuse the privilege of having this communications access. With Internet connections to your voters you may be able to cultivate a means of communication that your opponents will not have. I think e-mail will be the future of effective campaigning.

Election Weekend

Election weekend is actually the weekend before the Tuesday election. These are important dates because this is when you have to make your final push to be elected. The good news is that the public is now probably paying attention to the election process, and you can make an effort to make yourself stand out in the crowd. There are a number of things you can do to get noticed.

First, make sure that every sign is up and in good shape. This can be done early in the morning when you wouldn't be doing other campaign things. If you are running out of signs look for some of your signs located deep in sub-divisions or dead-end streets and move them out to better locations. You are looking for last minute visibility and high traffic areas will produce much more drive by interest.

You could also think about large banners that could be draped between trees or poles on private property. Banners are not allowed on public property or across public streets but they could be set up adjacent to such places to draw people's attention. You should think about all the ways you could get your name noticed. I knew one candidate that had a friend with a hot air balloon. The candidate had his name put on a huge sheet that was affixed to the existing balloon and when it rose in a parking lot it could be seen for many blocks in all directions. You could do a similar thing with the larger balloons you can buy in stores. Have your name put on them, filled with helium and tethered in a high traffic area for name recognition.

Years ago, many candidates would organize car-top carriers caravans to drive around town showing all the support a candidate had. They would drive down main-street with horns blaring and everyone taking notice. It was kind of an impromptu parade. While I haven't seen many such parades in recent years, there are other ways to gain attention.

Another way to garner attention is to get out and shake people's hands at the grocery store or the local bank. Saturdays are when people run about to take care of errands and get household chores done. Find a spot with high traffic patterns and get out there early to allow people to put a face with a name. If you have a commuter train stop in town, think about handing out leaflets to everyone boarding or getting off the train at the stop. With the election in people's minds they will stop and say hello, shake your hand and they will remember your face and name.

You may also want to have one more campaign literature drop just a few days before the election. This could be an all out blitz of all the neighborhoods in your voting district.

Your Final Campaign Delivery

The Election weekend is when you should make your final campaign literature delivery, either by mail or by hand if you have enough people to cover the neighborhoods involved. If you do plan to make the delivery by mail, pre-visit the post office and ask the postmaster what the timing should be. And be specific with what you are planning on doing. You don't want to drop the mail at the post office on that last Saturday before the election and find out the normal delivery would occur on Wednesday, the day after the election. That won't help you much at all.

You should show the Post Master what the mailing piece looks like and make sure it conforms to mail guidelines because you don't want to find out it has to be placed in an envelope or have a wafer seal on it at the last minute. Always ask about postage cost and delivery requirements, and what kind of timely delivery will be needed early in the campaign to prevent last minute surprises. The last thing you need to worry about is whether it will be delivered on time. By the way, Tuesday is too late as half the people will have gone to work and the other half will have already voted when the mail arrives.

If you are using volunteers for a home delivery make sure you have enough personnel to spread the job out. You don't want anyone to have to spend more than a couple hours covering a specific neighborhood, as they will balk at doing it, and they won't tell you. The last thing you want is to have someone say they will do it and then find the literature hidden in a dumpster behind the Seven-Eleven convenience store.

Way ahead of time, you should meticulously map out specific walking routes for the volunteers to cover, so that each area is assigned and no single area is too long or difficult. The route will usually be up and down a couple of streets perhaps 200–250 homes, which could be done in an hour or two. You could also match two people to a certain route allowing them to pace one another as they walk on each side of the street. This works well if you have young kids willing to go out with their parents. The parents can keep an eye on the children and the kids tend to make the parent move a little faster as they are racing down the street. Always give your workers detailed maps showing what streets they should cover and instructions on how to hang the literature on the house.

It should be noted that the U.S. Post Office frowns upon your using the mailboxes if a stamp has not been placed on the brochure. Frowns is actually not the correct term, its actually federal law that is involved so instruct your delivery people that they can't use the inside of the mailbox.

Provide your campaign workers with a bunch of rubber bands so that the brochure can be wrapped on or next to the mailbox, or on a door handle or some object at the door. You could encourage them to slide it into the door at eye level, or close the outer door on the brochure, half in and half out so that it can be seen. If none of that works I suggest they place it partially under the doormat or in a crack so that it won't blow away. But never in the mailbox.

You should also instruct your campaign delivery workers to use sidewalks and not jump over porch railings and cut across lawns to shorten distances, as that tends to aggravate people. You are trying to earn votes, not get voters to turn against you. If you explain the concept clearly to your workers they will understand why they need to take the longer route. While using the walks and driveways lengthens the route considerably, it makes common sense that you honor people's private property and flowerbeds.

Once the entire district has been covered with the literature drop, you should consider having an impromptu campaign party break at your house or headquarters. Hopefully you have a few dollars left, or you may have a sponsor that will help foot the bill, so organize one last campaign party for campaign workers as part of that last big push. Schedule it immediately after the final literature drop, so that people have a reason to come back to the house or office, and you will have the assurance that the last push actually occurred

This campaign gathering doesn't have to be anything fancy. It can be as simple as serving some beer for the adults, and soda for the kids, throwing some hot dogs and brats on the grill, and making sure there are enough lawn chairs to rest weary feet after the neighborhood walk-around. I ask people to bring the chairs when they come that morning to work. It is a great way to close out the campaign effort, thank your supporters and sit down and relax knowing you have given the effort a good run. If you can, save a few bucks in the budget so that you can make this effort to thank everyone. Then you wait, unless you want to make phone calls and try to convert a few more voters.

Election Day

On Election Day you should get up early because you have a few important things to before you vote for yourself. As early as possible make one more drive around the district to make sure all the yard signs are up and can be seen. This is the day you need as much visibility as you can muster. A sign knocked over or blown into bushes will not do you any good. You have to make sure they are all up and doing what you want them to do, at least for one more day.

In a 1982 campaign on election eve we had a major snowstorm that dumped 12 inches of snow in town. There had also been gale force winds and my signs were either buried or blown away. Knowing I had a problem, I got up at 4 am and replaced or fixed every sign by 7 am when the polls first opened. I think it made a big difference because my opponents were not out there fixing their signs; they were home sleeping in a warm bed. While turnout was lighter than expected due to the weather, I won that election and beat the incumbent, and I attribute part of that to my perseverance in getting the signs back up that freezing morning.

Pay special attention to the signs that are near or on the routes to the polling places. These are signs you have to have up and clearly visible on this final day. If you can locate them near the polling place and they legally conform to the local distance rules, make sure that they remain up throughout the day. It gives you one last shot at the voters and who knows, that last minute visibility could gain you a vote.

After you have done all you can in your final effort to campaign, I recommend a hot shower and cleaning up enough to make an appearance at the polling place. I always like to go early and be one of the first voters just to say that I was an early voter, reminding people to vote that may not have remembered. It never hurts to have other voters see you there. If your community has a daily newspaper, advise the editor that you are voting at 7 am and they may have a photographer there to cover you going into or coming out of the booth, and it could be in the afternoon addition.

Then you should check with your committee to help drive people to the polls. If your committee has done a good job, there will be a bunch of drivers already available and they will know who needs a lift, but checking in with them can offer another vehicle if needed. Then go do anything to get the campaign off my mind. Usually it's back to work for the day.

Poll Watchers

"Those who cast the votes decide nothing. Those who count the votes decide everything."

—Joseph Stalin

In America, one would like to think that Stalin's sentiment is a bit unfair, but after the problems we had with missing chads and electronic balloting there may be something to the statement. Thus it is imperative that you should monitor the polling places. A multitude of things can happen while the vote is being taken and once the tally is certified you will have little recourse to changing the outcome. To minimize potential problems and possible discrepancies you should plan to watch the polls. But you can't personally hang around all day as that would be considered politically improper. This can and should be done by your campaign committee members to make sure that you are actively listed and able to receive votes all day long. There may be multiple voting places depending on the number of wards that are actively electing candidates. You should have someone designated to watch each location to look for irregularities or problems that could adversely affect you. Poll watchers usually must officially designate themselves at the polling sites to legally be there.

You may ask, how it would be possible to lose votes on election day, but it could be the electronic machines are not working correctly, or the site loses power and people wishing to vote leave before the machines are repaired. That could mean you have to demand the machines be fixed or replaced immediately.

Your on-site poll watcher may notice that your opponent has signs placed right outside the door, or has brochures actually in the polling place. Unless challenged, the materials may be there all day long. These are campaign violations and create an unfair advantage for other candidates. In a case like this the poll watcher should bring the violation to the attention of an election judge and demand that the offending materials be immediately removed. The poll watcher shouldn't remove it themselves, but should insist upon removal, by the police if necessary. Such irregularities happen all the time!

Poll watchers can also help gage what the turnout is looking like and your committee can then decide if additional phone calling is warranted, or should they place people on street corners with billboards reminding people to vote. Your opponents won't let you know that the turnout is light because that may actually help them. Someone has to keep an eye on all the polling places.

At the end of the day these poll watchers should also watch how the votes are gathered and tallied. If manual tallies are taken they should monitor the counts and can often sit in close proximity to the official counters. They won't be able to touch any of the ballots but should note any irregularities or problems in the counting efforts. I have seen ballots tossed into garbage cans, dropped on the floor, and in one case actually torn up and disqualified without the benefit of a second judge's approval.

It's a good policy to have a number of people assigned to the polls because the day can be a long one and it can also be a rather boring time if everything is ship-shape and legal. Three or four people per location in 4-hour shifts, from 7:00 am to 10:00 pm should be enough. The late time slots are the most important to make sure all your votes and absentee ballots are counted correctly. By the way, you should not attempt to be a watcher yourself, as it is presumed you could influence voters. After you vote you should stay away from the actual polling places. Others should represent your candidacy.

Since you are not allowed to be near these counting efforts your poll watchers become your eyes and your ears. At the end of the day they monitor the official counts and call in the results for both you and your opponents because the official counts may not be released for hours. At your headquarters location, you should have a Campaign Tote Board made up with all the reporting precincts listed, and then wait for your people to call in the figures.

The official election judges have to report vote counts to Election Central not to your campaign headquarters. Having on-site observers speeds up the process. Many a Victory Party has gotten off to an early start when the called-in results showed you had a commanding lead. Your poll watchers can make for a less stressful evening.

One other thing to keep in mind is these poll watchers could assist you in identifying an irregularity that would negate the election if a challenge had to be made. If an irregularity is noted it should be brought to the attention of an official, documented by category and time, possibly photographed, and any other steps that would make it known that an irregularity has occurred. To get the problem noted you may even want to cause a scene to get the public and the press involved in the issue.

If you have to call for a challenge or a re-count of the election results, you may need the help of the public to make a challenge. Recently in one area election with new electronic balloting, the election officials ran out of the special paper needed for the electronic machines so hundreds of people were unable to vote and many gave up and went home. If you didn't have observers on hand the problem may never have surfaced and you would onluy wonder why the vote turnout was so light at that precinct. Line up a team of campaign workers you trust and have them be your eyes and ears.

The Campaign Party

You and your campaign workers have worked hard and deserve a party whether you win or lose. Your campaign workers will want to celebrate, or commiserate with you if you don't win. It is important that you finish the campaign with the same type of upbeat flair, so hopefully you saved a bit of money for beer, wine and snacks. That way everyone can have a good time for the effort they put into the campaign.

If you have watched national and state political campaigns you will always see that they have a hotel ballroom or hall reserved for the party. It's a big space because they have hundreds of people involved. You don't have to be that extravagant. If you have a recreation room or some space at your house that will do quite well if there aren't too many people invited. Keep in mind that everyone likes to celebrate with a winner so you may have more people than expected. If you think a large crowd might show up then find a hall or bar, or hotel ballroom that can accommodate the crowd.

In Sugar Grove, Illinois, my home community, there are multiple candidates running for a number of Village Board seats, and we all get together and rent the community house in town. Everyone volunteers to bring some type of food and snacks, and we all chip in for beer. In this manner we can handle a crowd if it materializes and no one has to expose their homes to a wild and raucous celebration. If no one shows up then the worst is that we have a lot of beer to consume!

At your election eve party, if you are the winner and new to the Board or Council, you should also expect that other Board members may drop by to congratulate you and perhaps court you to become a part of their coalition. You will find the political maneuvering will start almost immediately, before the ink on the ballots are dry, so keep your wits about you (watch your drinking) and don't make promises that you won't want to support after the glow has worn off. You may think I'm kidding when I say politicians will ask for your support on issues before they take their coats off, but it can and will happen.

But overall, this is an evening to celebrate, so enjoy the glow. You will also want to make some official comments to your fellow celebrants. It is important to remember to publicly thank everyone that helped you to become a candidate, and especially your spouse, and campaign committee as a group, and individually. These are the folks that supported you with time and perhaps money. Make them feel special and single out the real hero's. They will appreciate it and they will want to work for you again the next time. See, I already presume you will run again!

I even can offer you a joke to tell the crowd that will set the tone for the next few years. It goes like this:

An Elected Official is walking down the street one day and is hit by a truck and dies. The Official's soul arrives in heaven and is met by St. Peter.

St. Peter announces "Welcome to Heaven. Before you settle in, it seems we have a minor problem. We seldom see high Officials like you around these parts, so we are not sure just what to do with you. You will first have to spend one day in Hell and one day in Heaven. Then you can choose where you want to spend eternity"

St. Peter leads the Official into an elevator and pushes the down button to Hell. After a short trip downward, the doors open and the Official steps out into a beautiful pool area, next to a gorgeous golf course. Everyone seems to be happy and having a terrific time. He golfed and had the best score of his life, enjoyed caviar and lobster, and the softest feather bed anyone could ever have. The following morning it was time to go.

On the elevator going up the Official started calculating what heaven must be like. Upon arrival the Official finds beautiful clouds, and lots of nice people playing harps and lounging about, but little else. It was just a nice, quiet, dignified environment.

When St. Peter asks which location the Official wants to spend eternity in, it only takes a moment for the Official to choose the more exciting Hell. St. Peter smiles and opens the elevator door wishing his guest well.

The elevator trip down is quick and when the doors open the Official looks out on barren, scorched earth, with waste and squalor all about. The same people from the day before are there but working in the trash heap looking haggard, gaunt and destitute.

The smiling Devil walks up and throws an arm around the Official and says, "Welcome back, now get to work." The Official says, "I don't understand. Yesterday, I was wined and dined, ate Lobster and caviar, and had a great time. Now there is just this depressing wasteland?"

The Devil smiles and says "Yesterday we were campaigning. Today you voted for us!"

Note: If you use this joke, make sure you promise your term will be different, and you hope they will remind you of this joke every now and then!

If You Don't Win

If you don't win the election, it is just as important to hold that same campaign party. Remember the people who supported you still did the same amount of work; still delivered the brochures, put up the signs, and made the donations. A party is needed to acknowledge those efforts and let them know you appreciated their work. Also, remember that the next election is probably just around the corner and your team has already come together. So celebrate and hold your head high. Everyone deserves to be proud of the effort put forth.

There is one important additional task that should be performed when you don't win. You should call your opponent(s), perhaps as early as the evening of the election, once the results are known. You should call to officially concede and congratulate him or her on the victory. This is true even if it was a difficult campaign. You will bury the hatchet and show you are a true professional. Calling can be as simple as saying:

> **"Joe, I wanted to call and congratulate you on your victory and a great campaign. We had a good clean effort, discussed the issues, and I truly enjoyed the experience. I look forward to working with you in the future. Best of luck and congratulations again."**

That's all it takes and you will have shown you can take the high road in defeat. Sometimes this can be tough, but it shows that you are a good person, someone who can rise above adversity, and can move forward. Who knows, you may find a future ally. He or she may suggest that you get involved in some other way or may promise to support the issue you were in the race to resolve. The victor may be someone who will support you the next time you run. (See I'm already planning your next election and the ink on the ballots hasn't dried yet.)

I had to call Joe after a loss a couple years ago, and it hurt to do so, but I wanted to end the campaign on a positive note. Joe had been a good competitor, and he had won fair and square (by seven votes I might add, which made the call even more difficult). About six months later there was a vacancy on the Village Board due to another Trustee's resignation, and I applied for the interim position. Guess who was one of my supporters in discussion and voted in favor of my appointment. Joe supported me. I was back in the saddle serving on the Board with him. We are often allies on issues now and both take our responsibilities seriously.

Taking the high road in victory and defeat will allow you to take the field another day. So never turn your back on others and never burn bridges you may care to cross again in the future.

Campaign Post-Mortem

After Election Eve you should give yourself a rest for a week and then call your Campaign Committee together for a final post-mortem work session to pick the campaign apart. Make it more a social event than another campaign meeting. These individuals will have insights into what worked and didn't work in generating voter support. You should try to do this kind of analysis as soon as possible after the election while everything is fresh in your Committee's minds. Right after the campaign is over, before the dust really settles is the time to break down the campaign and figure out what went well and what didn't. Keep good notes because you will need these insights in a couple of years when you decide to run again.

Remember to file any of the Financial Reports that are required with the State or County, as no one will remind you of deadlines. This too is important especially if you decide to run again. Check with your bank about the status of you campaign account. If you have money left over you can use it up on the campaign party or post-mortem campaign committee meeting, or you can choose to leave it in place for a future election.

Also you may want to check your state campaign laws, about how excess funds can be utilized if you are stepping out of future races. At the state and national levels successful politicians have bankrolled these campaign treasuries into sizeable accounts over the years. In some cases they become rainy day funds for future campaigns. There are even laws that allow such campaign funds to eventually be disbursed to the candidate themselves to be used as they see fit. I've even seen them used as a retirement fund. I don't know how ethical it is to use these funds for personal use, since campaign donations are donated by people to support an issue or a candidate, not fund their retirement.

Then, you should gather up all your notes and store them away so they could be utilized in the future. Store all your signs in the basement, garage or attic in a dry place where all they will do is gather dust, so that you have a head start on your next campaign effort. Keep them in a corner where you can see them so you can gauge whether you have the fire in your belly to make another run at a future date.

Finally, look at the election as a learning experience, and start planning your next campaign adventure. Maybe it won't even be the same elected position you seek. It could be a different office that will be elected on a different cycle and could put you back in the game in a matter of months.

If You Have Won, Now What?

The first thing the morning after is to make sure that all your yard signs have been picked up. There is nothing worse then having old political signs lying around peoples' front yards. It becomes sloppy the moment the election is over. We have a community nearby that the town's government doesn't enforce their signage codes. They allow political signs to be placed on public property, almost every corner and on medium strips, almost anywhere the candidates can stick them. That makes for a sign proliferation that inundates the community. Then to make matters worse the community does not enforce the removal of the signs after the election. Some signs have stayed up for months after an election. You would think those candidates would take a little pride in their community and get them taken down. But many of them don't.

You should be a good candidate and remove them as soon as possible. These signs will cost you $5-6 dollars each so think of it as investing in your next run for office. When you have lots of signs, set up a Sign Retrieval Committee and actually do it the night of the election. I have always promised my sign home-owners that I will pull them quickly, and at 8:00 pm on election night after the polling places close they come down. Look at it as your first promise fulfilled to your supporters. Promptly collecting your signs also gives you a head start on the next campaign and saves you money. If you don't get them quickly people will pull them, tear them in half and throw them in the trash. Remember they cost over $5 a pop. You have to think ahead. You may run again in two or four years.

Another thing you should consider doing is printing up a quick "Thank You" for all the sign locations you had, that you could slip in the door as the signs are retrieved. Let the homeowner know that you appreciated his or her support and that you did clean up as you promised. It will go a long way with the voters and you'll have sign locations locked up for the future.

A victory signals a lot of work still needs to be done. You should start by thanking all the rank and file citizens who helped you win the election, including the people who made donations, put up signs, or called voters on your behalf. These folks probably were not at your Victory Party, so it is important to remember them. There are a number of ways to thank these folks. If you have a few bucks left take out an ad in the local newspaper and publicly thank everyone. If you have a good list of supporters and you have enough money to list their names, do it with a sincere thank you, as everyone likes to see their name in print when it isn't in the recently arrested column. It shows you care for all the people who had a hand in your victory. And remember you will be running again in a couple of years.

Keep track of peoples' names and addresses. With computers it is a snap to record and maintain all the names you have interacted with. Send these folks a short handwritten thank you note. It shows them you really appreciated their support and it will insure that they will remember you in the future. It takes some effort but that is what you have volunteered to do so its time you show your public you mean it.

If you have thousands of thank you notes to send out, do it with a printed letter, but personally hand write the salutation, *"Dear Mari"*, using their first names to let them know you are writing to them specifically. They will appreciate your consideration and feel as if they have a friend in high government places. That also means you may occasionally have them ask for a favor or request, but that goes with the turf. In most cases you will be able to assist these supporters, and establishing the relationship is worth the time and effort. These people helped you reach your goal. Don't forget them once you are a big shot.

Swearing-In and the First Meeting

A few weeks after the campaign you will be officially sworn into office usually at the start of one of the Board meetings. You may want to let your friends and family know about the swearing-in date as they will want to actually see it happen. Remember to bring a camera because the actual swearing-in will usually be with a Judge or the Mayor of the town, and it is your first official photo opportunity in front of the public. Up until now you had to manufacture press coverage, now they will be covering you as a public official.

You can also figure that the local press will want to do an interview for their publication so think about what you will want to say ahead of time. You might as well sound profound even though you don't know what is going on yet. Say you are honored to have been elected and look forward to working with this great group of elected officials. Then slip in another thank you for all your campaign supporters. It's a freebee so use the opportunity to advantage. The next time the press comes calling they will be asking tough questions and looking for real answers. Enjoy the friendly press experience while you can.

In this honeymoon period before the real work starts, set up a few meetings with the other government officials or the Mayor, and ask what they see as immediate issues. You may be asked to vote on an important issue at your very first meeting, as soon as 5 minutes after the swearing-in ceremony. Getting some insights into what's going on will make the first votes easier to handle and will make your first meeting less stressful. There has never been a "How to Act like an Elected Official" booklet given to new officials so it is kind of a baptism by fire.

I once took office and within seven minutes of being sworn in, was voting on a $38,000,000 dollar annual budget. I voted yes but didn't have a clue as to what I had just approved. Another time, I had to vote on a controversial issue that had been dividing the city, and I became the swing vote so everyone was watching me to see what I would do. This time I was prepared and had done my homework, knowing how I wanted to vote.

You should do as much background reading as possible. More likely than not, you will receive an Agenda, background and information on issues prior to that first meeting. Become familiar with the material and don't be afraid to ask questions of your new peers, before your sitting out in front of the public and on the record. Questions are tougher to ask in chambers because so many people may be listening. Your peers will gladly offer insights as they hope you will vote with them and become part of their group, coalition, party, machine, or cabal.

You should sort through all these issues and matters slowly and methodically, as you don't want to commit to things you will regret later. Take your time and reserve judgment until you have time to do your own research and think about how you want to vote. Don't be afraid to say you don't know yet, that you would like to look into the matter. No one will expect you to jump into the fray at your first meeting, but they will let you say what you want to say. So whatever it is you say, choose your words carefully.

Please know that it is OK to sit quietly for the first few meetings and not feel you have to comment or add discussion to every subject. Your peers will dissect the issues for you and all you initially have to do is attentively listen, and take good notes so that you can ask questions of them after the meeting. When actual votes need to be taken, don't be afraid to ask for guidance, or to abstain if you are unsure of how to proceed. As a rookie no one will demand you vote on all issues. But at the same time I would not recommend that you abstain too often because you were elected to take a position on issues.

There are many thoughts on how one should vote once elected to office, and it is worth discussing here.

> *"The things that will destroy us are:*
> *Politics without principle; Pleasure without conscience;*
> *Wealth without work; Knowledge without character;*
> *Business without morality; science without humanity;*
> *And worship without sacrifice."*
>
> **—Mahatma Gandhi**

There are two schools of thought on voting. One is that you have been elected to vote the wishes of your constituency, and you must do so in all cases. That is often called direct democracy or delegate democracy. The primary problem with this approach is, most of the time your constituents will not have an opinion on the myriad of subjects that you must vote on. Your constituents probably won't have an opinion on the cost or the size of sewer pipe, or whether the local festival should be allowed to have banner signs over the highway. They will want you to use your best judgment on these kinds of questions. They will only hold you accountable when the sewer pipe ruptures in front of their house and the banner sign is poorly made and garish in color marring the sunsets each night.

The other school of thought about voting is that the citizens voted for you to represent them, using your best judgment to work through the many issues that will come before the council. In a sense, this is why you spent so much time and effort trying to get the public to know you, to understand your views on important issues, and to trust you with their vote.

With this approach on voting you use your intellect and knowledge of issues to decide what is best for the community and its citizens, and then vote your conscience. This is called representative democracy and comes from a doctrine known as Edmund Burke's Principle.

Representative democracy and voting your conscience can also create problems when your conscience says it's the right thing to do for the community as a whole, but the decision will adversely impact certain people when that very busy street you are about to support, will run right past their bedroom window. You will always have NIMBY (not in my back yard) folks complaining about decisions that will benefit the greater good, but not them. They will have you believing it will be over their dead bodies. They don't want to hear about the greater good when they have to pay for it or can't sleep because of it. But it is important that you stand your ground.

> *"It may not always be easy, convenient, or politically correct to stand for truth and right, but it is the right thing to do. Always."*
>
> **—M. Russell Ballard**

You promised to uphold and protect the community as a whole and you have to make such decisions based on the greater community good. That's why President Harry Truman said the "the buck stops here" when he was talking about his decision on issues that arrived on his desk at the White House.

I have found that if you blend the two voting methods together, always trying to keep the general welfare and big picture in mind while at the same time trying to see individual viewpoints you can be effective most of the time. Always keep in mind:

"A Politician thinks of the next election; A Statesman thinks of the next generation."

—James Freeman Clarke

The secret is to realize early on that you will never please all of the people all of the time. For every decision you make for the common good, there will be certain individuals who will feel as if you have betrayed them. It is going to happen and if you are doing your political job correctly, you will invariably anger some people. It can't be helped, because in our democratic society, majority rules. You have to learn to deal with the angry voter who feels as if you have sold them out. Always remember the hundreds and perhaps thousands of other people who will benefit from your decision for a better quality of life.

The flipside of voting against a particular block of people is that if you anger enough people often enough, eventually you will find yourself challenged and un-elected in the next campaign, or even worse find yourself being recalled from office. But we have the carriage in front of the horse. You just need to do your homework, stay on top of issues, research how your constituents feel about important issues and then vote accordingly. If the majority of your voters like how you are voting, no individual or small group can force you out of office.

We talked earlier about a website for the political campaign. Once elected, that same website could be converted to stay in touch you're your constituents, discuss community issues, and poll voters on how they feel about various situations and issues. Think about a site that could act as your communications vehicle to reach your constituents. It may be a great way to stay connected.

While I rarely agree with a neighboring community Mayor's Blog website, he is doing an excellent job of gauging his constituents sentiments on all sorts of issues. He uses surveys and polls to promote his positions, sample citizen interests, and then uses all the information to help craft ordinances for his community. And I presume he is also capturing e-mail addresses of the people who write to him. He is building a stronger constituency.

An on-going website would give you an interactive means of sampling peoples' feelings about the subjects you need to vote on. Don't bore them with things like the size of water pipes and the sound decibels for traffic noise, but do zero in on major issues that will help you make decisions that require votes.

Years ago, I tried to keep the goodwill of a campaign going way past the election. When first elected Alderman in Wauwatosa, Wisconsin over 25 years ago, as a campaign promotion, I had created a 2-page campaign newsletter and promised to carry it forward as my District Newsletter after the election. I won the election and went on to publish the newsletter twice a year from that point forward. Sometimes I mailed it and hand delivered it others, which allowed me to meet even more people. I used it to raise issues with the voters and to seek their insights so I would know how to represent their interests. I received more calls than I wanted to, but then had a solid feeling on how to vote. The Newsletter allowed me to monitor voter interest and to keep my name in front of them throughout the term. It made getting re-elected easier the next time around. Now with websites available, you can create an electronic newsletter that can do the same thing and even can be delivered without cost.

Settling Into Office

When asked to name the chief qualities a politician should have.
"It's the ability to foretell what will happen tomorrow, next month,
and next year, and then explain afterward why it didn't happen."

—Sir Winston Churchill

After the Campaign Victory Party, after the swearing-in, and the first night's meeting, you will have a chance to actually become accustomed to the job. You will be asked to read all sorts of materials, examine budgets, and start the process of understanding how government functions. You won't need to learn everything at once so take your time and observe.

You might care to schedule meetings with your peers to have them advise you on what is going on. They will gladly share insights with you, but remember they will have their own spin on issues. It will be your job to de-cipher what it all means. Don't be too quick to align yourself with any party or group, as you may not like what you see after the alignment. Take your time and observe what is going on, how people vote on issues and listen to why they feel the way they do. You can learn a lot from your peers in a short time and it will be invaluable as you start to formulate your own thoughts.

Since you are now in the inner circle of local government, you can ask for documents and reports on any and all subjects that are before the official body. Don't be afraid to ask for them and read them. It may be confidential materials and it is important to honor the confidences, because usually sensitive materials can hurt someone or something if widely distributed. You might see documents that discuss a major land purchase and if known to the public too early would cause a real estate sell off. You might be privy to personnel issues that will affect the future job status of village employees. It is important that you honor confidences placed with you, as it will portray your ability to work with the elected officials for the common good.

Once you have settled in, talk to the Mayor and the Village Manager, and ask for a comprehensive tour of all government facilities, and introductions to the key Village or City employees. These will be the people you will be working with and will provide the bulk of the background information you will be looking at. And go visit with your friend the City Clerk who processed all your election papers and should know you by now.

If you are elected to a city position, you will want to meet the Public Works Director, who coordinates all major public services like water and sewer, roads and utilities. Ask to see all the public facilities that you never even knew existed, things like wells, pump houses, storage facilities for bulk materials, the fleet yard and public works building. Ask to see the maps that show all the water and sewer lines running beneath the street, how all the wells are interconnected and ask where all the weak points are in the system. Eventually you will need to know about water pressure capacities, flow ratios, the looping of pipelines to keep water moving and where all the waste goes and who is paying for the disposal.

These are all bread and butter issues that chew up tremendous amounts of the community budget, and you should know what these budget drains are all about early on. You will be shocked at what it costs to repave streets or put in new sewer lines. You will be surprised what a new dump truck with snowplow is going to cost and how much money goes into personnel and overtime when there is a 2:00 am call to handle a water main break on a Sunday evening in January. But it is important to know these things, so ask for the introductions and tour.

When it comes to Police and Fire, I have always asked for appointments with the Chiefs to ask for complete tours of their facilities and the district or city. Some of your greatest budget expenses will be in these public safety areas and you need to know what they are all about. Over the years I have asked to sit in on roll calls and meetings with police and fire personnel. I try to do a complete police shift drive-around every now and then to get a feel for what is going on in the community. Riding with an officer can offer a great look at safety issues and if the officer is willing to share information, you'll get a good feel for what problems exist and where future issues or concerns will come from. Plus you want to know your officers as they provide the safety and order in the village.

If your community is a growing one, you will have a Planning or Development Department, or both. You will want to understand how growth initiatives are going to affect populations, development needs, revenue resources, and how they will impact the budgets you are responsible for. These discussions will prepare you for the many important decisions you will be faced with concerning sub-divisions, schools, roads, infrastructure support and safety. You won't need to know all this stuff right away but it will allow you to better understand what you are reading about in all the reports you will receive and eventually have to vote on.

In my current community we are currently dealing with seven major home development builders creating 6,000 plus homes on over three thousand acres around the community. That is more physical space than the whole community presently covers now. As these neighborhoods are developed, the Village will provide police and fire, street maintenance and snow plowing with little income coming in until homes are built and eventually go on the tax roles.

While these new homeowners eventually contribute to the budget coffers, initially they put tremendous strain on the community budget because property taxes are always collected a year in arrears. So the community provides service for the better part of 12 to 18 months before one new tax dollar arrives. Understanding these facts and processes will be invaluable in addressing issues that you will encounter.

Try and get to know all your city personnel, as it will allow you to have better insights into the mysteries of government. As you have probably heard, government moves rather slowly. That is partially because government is held to a higher standard of ethics because it is utilizing the publics' money to work for the common good. Things rarely move quickly because issues need to be pre-posted for pubic scrutiny, comment and lots of discussion. Public hearings are held and financial impact statements and a multitude of reports have to be carefully reviewed so that funding options are clearly understood. Again, all this is done because of the use of the publics' funds. And you are the arbiter of these monies for the voters who elected you.

Good Luck, Get Going!

Well, its time to get to work. We can talk about all these things ad nauseum, but it will be better for you, the victorious candidate, to just immerse yourself in the process of government. Its time to dive in and learn all these things on your own. I guarantee you will enjoy the experience, just as I have over the last twenty-five years. I take great pride in contributing my time and effort to my community. I'm sure that you will too!

I hope that this "Getting Elected" information book has been helpful in organizing your thoughts on how to get elected. I also hope you will experience victory in your campaign effort. I would love to hear that you were successful in your campaign effort. Please e-mail me at gettingelected@yahoo.com. Let me know how it went, or if I could offer any advice to help you on this wonderful journey. Good Luck!

Glossary of Terms

Absentee Ballot. If a qualified voter is disabled, elderly, or will be traveling on election day, that person may obtain an absentee ballot ahead of time, vote, have his vote sealed and counted on election day. Absentee ballots are available, usually from the Clerk, up to some official deadline day. After that day which may be 10 days before the election, the voter would have to show up and vote to be counted. Often these Absentee ballot requests can be pre-distributed by the candidate or committee when such voters are identified.

At Large. An at-large race is an election throughout the entire jurisdiction, rather than in smaller sections, wards or precincts. The Mayor would run in the whole community, whereas an Alderman may only run in one district or ward. Races that do not have districts or wards will have candidates running at-large throughout the community. In this case, citizens from throughout the community vote for a slate of candidates that will represent the whole community.

Board of Elections. This is the official body that conducts, administers and warrants the election laws, including finance, ethics and regulations. This Board may be at the City, County or State level.

Budget. In terms of the election it is a laundry list of all the potential income and expenses that are contemplated in the process. It can be rather simple or very complex only dictated by the amount of contributions and the actual campaign expenses. It should be detailed enough to assist in overall planning of time, energy and money.

Campaign. The official public race for elective office. The term embodies all that is related to the effort to win an election.

Campaign Manager. Also known as the Campaign Chairman, this person is usually in charge of all elements of the campaign, allowing the candidate to meet the people, ring the doorbells and not get bogged down with all the administrative requirements of the campaign.

Campaign Timeline. This is a critical tool for any campaign that outlines the overall plan for the candidate's elective process. Think of it as a detailed calendar showing all reporting deadlines, important events, required meetings, and strategies that will be employed to keep the candidate and committee on track.

Census district. This is the geographic/demographic information of the campaign boundaries, outlining where the campaigning must go on. The census information will offer data on the target area and will assist in understanding the demographics of that jurisdiction. This information can be found in the library, on the US Census website and may be available at the clerk's office. There is also demographic information available for each zip code and district.

Circulator of Petitions. This is the designated person or persons who pass and circulate your nominating papers on your behalf. These can be people on your committee who have volunteered to secure signatures. They often must officially sign the Petition as the person circulating, and then attest that they personally witnessed the signatures being written on the form. In most cases a candidate can also be a Circulator.

Constituency. This the body of voters that resides in a particular precinct, ward, district or elective area. Once elected to office the official will often call the voters represented his or her constituency.

Contribution. Any donation made to the candidate to assist in the election effort. These donations can be cash, checks or in-kind donations. Most states require that all donations in any form be formally recorded on the Campaign Finance Reports.

Crossover voting. Qualified voters may choose to temporarily change official party status, or step outside of party ranks, by crossing over and voting for a candidate in a different party.

District. District refers to the official geographic boundaries of the elective office being sought. The term can be synonymous with ward, precinct, township, parish, town, city, county, or state depending on the locale and the office being sought.

Election statistics. All past election results are maintained on file (computer records) for purpose of analysis, and can be broken into categories of party, district, primary and final votes, geographic region, and political party. These statistics are valuable in understanding voting patterns and planning a campaign based on identifying probable real voters who will actually turn out for the election.

Elector. A person who is officially registered, and thus entitled to vote in an election. A voter must pre-register in order to become a valid elector and must re-register anytime their address should change in order to qualify.

Ethics Report. As part of a campaign a candidate may have to sign an ethics statement that they will abide by basic rules of the election.

Ethnic Voter. A voter who identifies himself with a certain group of people based on religion, nationality, race or some other sub-culture distinction. A candidate may find these voters tend to vote more in a block and if a rapport can be established with them, the candidate might earn a favorable level of support.

Expenditure. Any use of campaign funds to pay for expenses incurred in the campaign to assist candidate. All of these expenditures must be recorded on financial reporting forms and submitted for official records.

Filing Deadlines. These are the official dates that nominating papers and official Petitions, possibly financial reports, and other official forms must be filed to maintain candidacy status according to state law. Missing such deadlines will end a campaign immediately.

Finance Chairman. This is the campaign manager handling all financial matters for the candidate. This person must usually officially file as the Finance person and must meet certain deadlines as well. This person usually will coordinate all financial matters on behalf of the candidate and file all necessary papers as required by law.

General Election. This election tends to be a major one usually associated with national elections in November. Often there will be elective races in national state and local regions all on the ballot at the same time. Typically this is when the largest number of voters turn out. State and local elections often do not draw as much interest and voting.

High-profile election. This is an election that draws a lot of interest, perhaps a presidential campaign or major state races. The press follows what is going on and raises the interest level of voters causing a much larger turnout. A good example of a high profile election would be Hillary Clinton's Senate election in New York. If you were running as a candidate at the local level you could expect that more people will show up to vote and that may work in your favor if you have good name recognition.

Independent candidate. A person not formally aligned with any formal political party who chooses to run without such support. An independent candidate can benefit by not aligning with a party, but then does not receive the financial support that a party can lend to its candidates. Many local elective offices are non-partisan where no party affiliation is needed or even suggested.

Independent voter. This is similar to the above independent candidate in that the voter has not aligned with any formal party designation and as such has no party obligation to vote accordingly. People claiming they are independent have been on the rise suggesting that perhaps they have been less than satisfied with party affiliation.

Low-profile race. This is a race or election that does not generate a lot of public interest or where voters have little interest in who is running or the office itself, like the Village Clerk, Recorder of Deeds, or the Coroner. Referendums often fall into this category. If a candidate is running in such an election getting people to the polls may be difficult. Knowing that, and putting in some extra effort may allow the candidate to win even with a low turnout.

Loyalty Oath. Often a candidate will be asked to officially file a statement of candidacy and as a part of that form there may be a Loyalty Oath that also needs to be filed. It simply states that a candidate swears allegiance to the laws of the land, the United States Government, the State, and the locality of the election.

Name Recognition. The candidate's efforts to get his name out in front of the public and gain visibility. Name association can win elections if you have an easy name to remember, an ethnic name, or a very long name. The secret is to have the voters associate the name with the office when they get inside the voting booth.

Nominating petitions. The official documents often called Nominating Papers that are circulated to voters to petition for your candidacy. A certain number of signatures are required to get your name on the ballot. These forms are obtained at the Clerk's or Elections office and must be turned in by a defined deadline day and time to be on the ballot.

Non-partisan. Means you are not affiliated with any official political party. In a non-partisan election, party affiliation is not required on the part of the candidates, and qualified voters do not have any party voting restrictions. This is often the case at the local level. While you may be a party member yourself, in a non-partisan race you do not have to declare your party affiliation.

Notary Public. An official office and person that is empowered by the state to witness that documents are actually signed and verified. Individuals become Notaries and can offer their services as a witness, for a small fee. They usually have an official seal that is authorized by the state that is used to authenticate the signatures and filings. A Notary Public is used to verify that Nominating papers, financial filings and other documents have been officially presented. Notaries can be found in law offices, real estate offices, banks and usually in the city clerk's office.

Off-year election. This election is held in reoccurring years when no high-profile offices for President, Governor or Senate are being filled. Off-year elections are usually more regional or local and often are held in the spring of the year.

Open primary. If a large number of candidates are running for office a primary may be scheduled to elect the official candidates of the parties. In this case only party members vote for candidates on each side of the political slate. Both parties may have open primaries to identify their respective candidates that would allow the public to crossover and vote in the opposite party's election.

Political Action Committee (PAC) This is a special interest group that is interested in having a political impact on an election. The PAC will contribute money and perhaps help in supporting candidates they believe in. These PAC's are governed by campaign finance law and have their own regulations, filing reports and requirements to operate in the political arena. Interacting with PAC's involves additional scrutiny so that all financial matters are recorded appropriately.

Political Map. This is a specific map of the electoral districts in a community with the precincts and wards clearly designated. Such a map becomes an important tool to use in organizing an effective campaign strategy. This map will show you where all the corners of the district are. Often map lines will cut right down the middle of streets, or through neighborhoods. It is important to clearly understand where the lines of the districts and wards are located.

Polling Place. This is an official site where qualified voters actually show up to vote for the candidates of their choice. There may be numerous polling places in a community and they are often found in public buildings, schools, fire stations and libraries. The voting machinery is temporarily moved to these sites for the election.

Poll watchers. These are campaign workers who observe the election polling sites throughout the day to insure that a fair and impartial vote is taken. They represent their candidate and make sure people are able to vote, that machines function correctly, that no one campaigns in or around the polling place and most important they monitor the final voting counts and validation of the result. They become a candidate's eyes and ears throughout election-day as the candidate is not allowed on site except to vote.

Precinct. The smallest electoral voting area in a district, often a part of larger wards. It is common that a precinct will have its own polling place located in the specific geographic area.

Precinct committeeman/woman. Within political parties each precinct will have its own party member (both democrat and republican) who coordinates the affairs within the precinct. These are often appointed or volunteers who organize the party effort to turnout the vote on election-day.

Primary election. This is an election held prior to the general election to narrow the choices for voters. Parties have a primary election to select a candidate rather than having multiple candidates on the ballot. In non-partisan elections the community may have a primary to narrow the number of candidates on the ballot, rather than having ten or more. Those gathering the most votes in the primary move on to the general election. A primary is an important election if you have multiple candidates all taking some of the vote. You have to pass the first hurdle before moving to the second race.

Referendum. A referendum is a formal petition made by an individual or a group to officially place something before the voters of a locality. A referendum is a direct popular vote asking voters to endorse or reject some action that is contemplated. Referendums can ask binding questions with the vote determining an action, and non-binding referendums which would only suggest how the voters feel about some important matter before the public. Often taxing bodies would need the approval of a voter referendum to raise taxes or make a change in the tax rates to be charged.

Registered voter. This is a person who has filed and qualified to become a voter. It does not mean that they actually vote, only that they are entitled to if they show up.

Restrictive Covenant. As used in local government this is a property term related to pre-agreed upon rules that are imposed on a body of people. Often a subdivision or a particular neighborhood will have special rules that have been imposed upon all who live there. These restrictive covenants are often agreed upon when the development is first annexed into a community, or when some action is requested by a number of citizens. An example would be a covenant disallowing in-ground pools or out buildings in a particular area.

Special election. This is an election that is not normally scheduled in the spring or fall, usually for a specific purpose such as a referendum, a tax levy, or to fill a vacancy in office because the next regularly scheduled election is too far off to wait.

Statement of Candidacy. This is usually an official document that is required to place a name on the ballot for an election. Certain conditions are outlined in order to qualify to become a candidate for public office. This form often includes an Oath of Allegiance, and financial reporting requirements.

Supervisor of Elections. Depending on state, this may be an official office, and a person that oversees the entire election process in the state, county or locality. This Official is charged with the responsibility of authenticating candidates petitions, coordinating all filings required by law, overseeing the actual election day process, and insuring that all parties have a fair chance to participate in the elective process.

Swing Precincts. These sub-district areas can cause an election outcome to change because of their voting independence, their group alliance, or because they are voting like a single block. Swing voters act the same way at an even smaller unit level.

Thomas F. Renk

Tom Renk has been active in local government in two different states for the past twenty-five years. He first got started in public service in 1977 when he was appointed to the Wauwatosa, Wisconsin Board of Zoning Appeals after losing an election for Alderman. He later was elected Alderman in that city serving from 1982 to 1986, until his family moved to Illinois.

In Naperville, IL., he assisted a number of candidates with their campaigns for public office. In 1997 he built a new home in Sugar Grove, IL. and decided to run for an open Village Trustee position. He ran a textbook campaign and was elected as Trustee earning the most votes of all four candidates. Four years later he lost that position by seven votes, but was re-appointed a few months later when another Trustee stepped down. In 2005 he ran again for Trustee and came in first in a field of five candidates.

He currently resides in Sugar Grove and represents the Village as a Trustee. Sugar Grove is a small but fast growing community on the western edge of metropolitan Chicago. It is a community dealing with thousands of new home starts, fast growing schools and all sorts of infrastructure issues that keeps him active and involved.

He is a graduate of the University of Wisconsin-Whitewater with a Bachelor of Science degree in Political Science and Economics. He is an Executive Vice President of Association Enterprise, Inc., a trade association management company in Naperville, Illinois. As an Executive Director of a number of national and state non-profit organizations in a variety of industries, he coordinates memberships, databases, publications, government affairs, meetings and trade shows for his client accounts.

I would like to thank Karen, my wonderful spouse of 36 years, my best friend for the past 40 years, and the best business partner I've ever had, for her constant support, her true inspiration, and loving guidance. Her political insights have always been right on the money. And I think she always voted for me!

I would also like to thank my three children, Courtney, Michael, and Kate for their support and political help through the years. They were the reason I wanted to get involved in community. Also special thanks to Courtney, who inspired this book with her crayon "Elect Courtney's Daddy" signs over 25 years ago.

Then I would like to thank my parents, Ralph and Peggy Renk, for showing me at a young age what politics and community service was all about. They offered me inspiration by setting great examples of what good, involved citizens should be.

Also, I would like to thank my fellow elected officials, both current and past, for their guidance, support, direction and fellowship. I have been constantly amazed and inspired by their dedication to community. This includes all my challengers over the years, who helped to make me a better candidate and a stronger elected official. They taught me how to campaign, and how to win confidently, and how to lose gracefully. In many ways they helped me write this book. Hopefully, it will now help others to get elected in their communities.

Finally, I would like to hear from you, especially candidates who have benefited from this book. You can reach me at getting elected@yahoo.com, or at trenk@sugar-grove.il.us. I would like to hear about your successes and your temporary setbacks. Perhaps we can compare notes and I can offer some insights you may not have thought about. And finally, the best of luck on your quest for public office.

Tom Renk

978-0-595-39667-2
0-595-39667-4

Printed in the United States
55554LVS00003B/103-141